SCOTLAND
SINCE
PREHISTORY

SCOTLAND SINCE PREHISTORY

Natural Change
and
Human Impact

edited by

T C Smout

**SCOTTISH
NATURAL
HERITAGE**

SCOTTISH CULTURAL PRESS

First published 1993
Scottish Cultural Press
PO Box 106, Aberdeen AB9 8ZE, Scotland UK

A British Library Cataloguing-in-Publication Data
record for this book is available from the British Library

ISBN: 1 898218 03 X

The publisher acknowledges assistance
from Scottish Natural Heritage towards the publication
of this volume

Typeset by Scottish Cultural Press
Printed and bound by BPCC-AUP Aberdeen Ltd

CONTENTS

FIGURES

PLATES

BP   Before Present (ie before the 1990s)

ix

CONTRIBUTORS

Hugh Cheape, National Museums of Scotland, Queen Street, Edinburgh

Kevin J. Edwards, School of Geography, University of Birmingham, Edgbaston, Birmingham

Stratford P Halliday, The Royal Commission on Ancient and Historical Monuments of Scotland, Sinclair House, 16 Bernard Terrace, Edinburgh

J John Lowe, Centre for Quaternary Research, Department of Geography, Royal Holloway, University of London, Egham, Surrey

Alexander Mather, Department of Geography, University of Aberdeen, St Mary's, Elphinstone Road, Old Aberdeen

Alasdair Roberts, Educational Studies, Northern College, Aberdeen

John S Smith, Department of Geography, University of Aberdeen, St Mary's, Elphinstone Road, Old Aberdeen

Chris Smout, Institute for Environmental History, University of St Andrews, Fife

David W Summers, Game Conservancy, Fordingbridge, Hampshire

Camilla Toulmin, Director, Drylands Programme, International Institute for Environment and Development, London

Graeme Whittington, School of Geography and Geology, University of St Andrews, Fife

FOREWORD

Magnus Magnusson

Naturam expellas furca, tamen usque recurret
You can drive out Nature with a pitchfork, but she will always
make a comeback (Horace)

One might say that Horace was the classical prototype environmentalist. On his farm in the Sabine hills beyond Tivoli he created landscapes as lyrical as his odes, and practised pastoralism with the 'studied felicity' (*curiosa felicitas*) of his poetry. He was Augustan man *par excellence*: he celebrated Nature not in the raw but dressed in manicured seemliness, trained to man's bidding by kindness rather than by brute force. Yet, as he wryly noted, once the pitchfork is laid aside, Nature comes into her own again.

The story of man's relationship with the environment is the burden of this absorbing collection of studies. Modern scholarship is doing much to broaden our knowledge of the interaction between human society and natural change since earliest prehistoric times down to the present day: indeed, the study of environmental history has become an important academic discipline in its own right.

It has also given rise to the intriguing concept of 'cultural landscape', a relatively recent term coined to indicate a specific role which man has played in the evolution of a particular area, both through managing the resources of the land to meet human needs, and through expanding the built elements of the landscape. It is an evolution which has been, partly at least, conditioned by man's response to the limitations and opportunities of the natural environment of a place.

For Scottish Natural Heritage this is of crucial significance. There is not much that is 'natural' about the natural heritage: 'semi-natural' is no doubt a more accurate if more prosaic term. Our view of the natural heritage encompasses its cultural and historical dimensions as well as the more obvious factors of wildlife, habitat, and landscape; mankind is part of nature rather than separate from it, part of the natural order.

We regard the creative manifestations of our interaction with the rest of the natural world as integral parts of the natural heritage. Our concern with wildlife, habitats, landscapes and with natural processes is inseparable from our concern for and interest in human activity within the community of life.

It is clearly important to know as much as we can about the extent and nature of this 'cultural' dimension, because the business of maintaining and enhancing the natural heritage is essentially a matter of understanding and managing change. The natural heritage is never static. It is in a constant state of dynamic change as a result of a wide range of environmental factors, whether caused by climatic variation or geomorphological activity or man's increasingly puissant pitchfork.

Nature's time clock is relatively slow. Even those more cataclysmic changes of drifting continents and species extinctions are measured in millions of years rather than millennia. In comparison, man's intervention is short and brutal. He has removed the virgin forest, introduced alien species, established domestic hybrids, and fundamentally changed the landscape in a few millennia. Indeed, some actions can be achieved virtually overnight; but to correct them may take many generations. In other words, the repair may take at least an order of magnitude of time longer than the deed.

One of the great fascinations of the study of nature change is to determine whether it is continuous and in one direction, or whether there is a cyclical effect. Unlike the efforts of man's pitchfork, we have to ask the question as to whether nature is as self-repairing as Horace suggested. The answer, perhaps, is *yes* only when the impact of the natural and man-induced change has not resulted in catastrophic or irreparable change. In contrast, all too many of the changes brought by man may appear to be irreversible.

What is clear from the chapters in this volume is the importance of this subject of environmental history. We need greater clarity and less ambiguity. For example, was peat formed by climatic change or by man's interaction? We could profit from further work from the environmental record. What were the population level and distribution of our indigenous species in recent centuries? We could profit from deeper study of the written record. These and many other subjects are not only all valid areas of study but vitally relevant issues for increasing our understanding and prompting deeper consideration of the interaction between man and his environment.

So it is a particular pleasure to welcome this volume, the first fruits of the newly-founded Institute for Environmental History at the University of St Andrews. It is a book for lay and learned alike. The individual chapters all cast a refreshing new light on areas of resource-management such as farming and forestry and fishing, in both the distant and the immediate past, which are all matters of urgent present interest and current controversy.

It is good to see received ideas being re-examined and, if necessary, re-defined. This book challenges us all to look again at our own preconceptions and prejudices—even our prejudices about midges, forsooth!—and to be prepared to adapt our own attitudes to change in the light of changing times and ideas.

Magnus Magnusson KBE
Chairman
Scottish Natural Heritage
November 1993

INTRODUCTION

Chris Smout

Environmental history arose as an international discipline from a number of roots. Archaeologists after the Second World War discovered that phytology, the science of pollen analysis, and allied technologies, could enrich their understanding of the economy of very remote societies. Historians and historical geographers, influenced by the ecological movement of the last few decades, began to realise that the history of humanity is not about the conquest of nature, but of accommodation to it:

> The leitmotiv of Western history known as "our increasing control over nature" is actually an absurd, barefaced oxymoron. Nature has always been in total control, both in the basic, merely logical sense that the characteristics of Nature which make it inhabitable for us can no wise be taken for granted, and in the more disturbing, factual sense that Nature has already considerably reduced our domain. (Duncan 1991)

The same influences set off a quest by philosophers and cultural historians to explore the intellectual origins of modern ideas about the role and place of nature in human life.

The subject thus has several points of departure and encompasses several academic interests, but environmental history is always about human interaction with the natural world. It differs from economic history in that the main focus is not upon the conditions which produce economic growth or the material enrichment of society, but upon the environmental impact of the human exploitation of natural resources. Characteristically, it is about the impact of agriculture on the history of soils and of natural woodlands, about the effect of hunting on animal stocks and of grazing on native vegetation, and about the changes wrought by industry, forestry, mining, transportation and urbanisation. It is also about the manner in which natural phenomena affect human society, in the way in which floods, alterations in sea levels, volcanic explosions or climatic changes, for example, alter the patterns of resource use by making land uninhabitable or by providing new land to inhabit. And it is about our attempts to discover, explain, understand, cope with and appreciate nature, that is, about the anthropology and cultural history of human understanding of the world around us. It can deal with very ancient times, with societies that existed millenia in the past, or it can deal with very modern subjects, the environmental impacts and conflicts associated with modern economic developments.

Does it have an ideology? Economic history has been accused of a triumphalist tone, of chronicling a conquest of nature always for the best. Environmental historians have equally been portrayed as having a bias towards gloom and doom, of showing a natural world degraded always for the worst. It can be argued that economic history is the child of the optimism of Adam Smith, and environmental history of the sensibilities of Jean-Jacques Rosseau, whom Voltaire accused of wishing us back to the cave on all fours (La Frenière 1990). To be fair, however, modern economic and social historians are often very aware of the limits, costs and ambiguities of growth, and environmental historians concomitantly aware of the innumerable occasions in which a human sense of self-preservation, good stewardship or sheer accident have kept development within sustainable bounds. It is easy to hear in the pages of the *Environmental History Review* the tones of ecological concern, even occasionally of polemical engagement, just as there is sometimes discernible in the pages of the *Economic History Review* the even loftier tones of economists admonishing the world. Though we may find it hard to resist, it is nevertheless no part of the job description of historians of any kind either to rebuke the past or foretell the future.

We do, however, have a relevant and urgent task to describe and analyse the environmental history of past centuries as exactly as we can, and that for a straight political reason. Unless we do it right, others will make up history for us in order to create myths to justify this or that political, economic and environmental programme of their own. Such myths can have great power to guide and to mislead. Since everything to do with the environment at the end of the twentieth century is at root a politically contentious matter (Pepper 1984), the need for good scholarship in searching but accessible environmental history is a matter of the most pressing importance.

The concept of environmental history is, however, less familiar in Europe than it is in America and Australia, and probably less so than in Asia and Africa. The reason is not far to seek. The impact of white settlement on areas of superficially pristine wilderness only two or three hundred years ago, in areas like eastern North America and southern Australia, was so enormous that it invited substantial historical investigation. At first, this was along the conventional lines of economic history, in its subdivision of agricultural history, but with burgeoning interest in anthropology and ecology, a much more interdisciplinary approach was seen to be appropriate. Historical geographers, especially of Australia, cut the first sod (Meinig 1962; Williams 1974). Environmental history demonstrated the wilderness not to have been so pristine after all, but to have been modified over the millenia by American Indians and Australian Aborigines; at the same time the impact of Europeans was understood to have had costs and implications greater than those perceived by the older school of economic historians (Cronan 1985; Bolton 1981; Whitelock 1985; Lines 1991). In America, the search has since widened to describe the impact of a great city on its surrounding environment (Cronan 1991), and the implications of the interface between

Privileged Position

Catherine Orr

Sitting behind people in buses
you notice eye lashes –
how long they are,
and the way earrings pinch,
and the bristly route
the clippers took,
and the pluke.

It's a private view
in a public place.
Motorists miss it,
the almost illicit
chance to inspect
that most vulnerable part,
the back of the neck.
It's a position of maximum trust
sitting behind anyone in a bus.

Scottish **Book** Trust

NATIONAL
POETRY DAY
Thursday 4 October 2001

Post a poem today!

Privileged Position
© Catherine Orr

No.6 in a series of 8

Collect the rest! Send a 1st class sae to NPD 2001, Scottish Book Trust, 137 Dundee Street, Edinburgh EH11 1BG

www.scottishbooktrust.com

women's history and environmental history (Merchant 1989). The case study approach towards nineteenth and twentieth century study conflicts over environmental questions filled the pages of the *Environmental History Review* (which in 1990 significantly changed its name from *Environmental Review*), and inspired several monographs (e.g. Coates 1991; Frome 1992). Intellectual historians and philosophers struck a vein of gold in investigating the significance of the Judaic-Christian attitude towards the environment (Glacken 1967; White 1967; Passmore 1980), and in wider accounts of the attitude to nature, including the rise of an American wilderness ethic exemplified by figures like Thoreau, John Muir and—in our own century —Aldo Leopold (Nash 1973; Worster 1977; Oelschlaeger 1991). By the 1990s, courses in environmental history were being offered in at least five American universities, including Yale and Berkeley, and humanistic courses were being offered at as many Australian universities, especially Adelaide and Monash. Good environmental history was being written in India (e.g. Guha 1990; Rawat 1991; Gadgil and Guha 1992), and Chinese scholars were seeing the subject as offering an escape from the intellectual blinkers of Maoism (Hou 1990).

In Great Britain, historians of Africa, Latin America and Asia saw the relevance of environmental history in their fields, and a few even became engaged in its research (see e.g. Anderson and Grove 1987; Mackenzie 1990; Grove 1992). Cambridge University Press established a series, 'Studies in Environment and History' that published work of international scholars on particular countries, for example, the United States (Williams 1989; Silver 1990) and Brazil (Dean 1987), as well as an admired study of ecological imperialism on a world canvas (Crosby 1986) and an anthology of exemplary studies from across the whole field (Worster 1988). But it is a remarkable fact that neither of the editors, nor any of the six members of the first advisory board, were British scholars, or interested in British history.

At first sight, therefore, it looks as if British scholars have fallen behind their international colleagues in recognising the linkages between the natural environment and their own history. Certainly in Britain true wilderness is so much a matter of the remote past that it has never acted as an inspiration to historians. Instead, they left the study of human interaction with the environment to economic (especially to agricultural) historians, and to historical geographers, each generally focussed on problems of development rather than problems of impact.

However, this was by no means the entire story. The development of phytology (pollen analysis) and dendrochronology (the study of tree rings) gave rise to extremely fruitful interdisciplinary work linking archaeologists, botanists and geographers in the study of the earliest human environments in Britain, in which it was discovered that stone-age, and particularly bronze-age and iron-age peoples, had already made a very considerable impact on the primaeval wilderness, long before the dawn of the Christian era (summarised in Simmonds and Tooley 1981). W J Hoskins, an inspiring rogue elephant among economic historians, and Oliver Rackham, a rogue elephant among botanists, who turned historian, covered the ground of mediaeval and early modern history with important and highly readable studies of the English landscape and of English woodland, showing how they still bore detailed evidence of past human working practices, and how such things as hedges and woods were artefacts as valid for their resonances of past social life as any scheduled historic building (Hoskins 1965; Rackham 1980, 1986; for a French equivalent woodland study, see Bechman 1984). The notion of a 'cultural landscape', popular among Scandinavian geographers and their British colleagues, came increasingly to the fore both in terms of land-use history and of ideological meaning (Birks et.al. 1988; Cosgrove 1984; an important Danish study is Olwig 1984). At the modern end of the time spectrum, John Sheail in particular explored the rise of the modern conservation movement in Britain (Sheail 1976, 1981), the history of British ecology and some of the collisions between ecological science and modern industrial interest (Sheail 1985, 1987). Peter Brindlecombe tackled the history of London's air pollution since the Middle Ages (Brindlecombe 1987). There was a parallel to American work on the wilderness idea in the works of Raymond Williams, Hugh Thomas, and David Allen, exploring in different ways attitudes in England to the natural world since the sixteenth century (Williams 1973; Thomas 1983; Allen 1976). Although scarcely recognised as such, by the 1990s the varied lights of environmental history were beginning to glow in a number of areas of British study.

In Scotland we are just starting to identify environmental history as valid and distinctive, despite very pioneering work on the aspects of species and vegetation history in the nineteenth century (Harvie-Brown 1879, 1881, 1892; Nairne 1891) and James Ritchie's remarkable monograph on human impact on the fauna, at least half a century ahead of its time (Ritchie 1920). Scotland has, however, been a theatre for phytologists and environmental archaeologists since the 1950s (see for example, Birks 1972), and recent work by archaeologists in particular has emphasised the concerns of environmental history (Edwards, forthcoming; Macinnes and Wickham-Jones 1992; Price 1982): there has similarly been recent work in land use and forestry studies (Bachell 1991; Dickson 1993; Tipping 1993) and on the history of a Scottish conservation ethic (Smout 1990). This volume is offered as a further contribution to the emergence of environmental history as a fledged discipline in Scotland.

All but one of the chapters originated as papers to the first conference of the Institute for Environmental History of the University of St. Andrews, held at the Scottish Natural Heritage countryside centre at Battleby, Perth, in December 1992, with financial support from the Royal Society of Edinburgh, Historic Scotland, British Petroleum plc and SNH itself. The purposes of the meeting were straightforward—to demonstrate the breadth and vitality of environmental history in Scotland, to sketch out in a series of important areas what is the current state of understanding in the subject, to indicate agendas for the future, and to act as a springboard for future conferences with further and more detailed explorations. In a one-day meeting, only limited areas could be covered—very obviously, no attempt has been made to discuss the history of environmentalism in Scotland, or to tackle recent 'case studies' of conflict. The papers had a large enough task as it was, to survey the general area of human impact on the natural environment of Scotland from the mesolithic to the present.

They range widely, beginning with John Lowe's opening account of the omnipresent character of environmental change throughout geological time, reminding us that humanity is placed in a dynamic, not a balanced or a static, natural world; and concluding with Camilla Toulmin's account of the Sahel, there to remind us that problems of cultivating marginal land which have loomed so large in Scottish history exist also in very different climates and times, and to hear her lesson that local peoples often know better than experts how to treat fragile ecosystems.

The nine chapters between are all specifically Scottish. Graeme Whittington explains the significance of phytology, and of its findings in several Scottish situations. Kevin Edwards takes a series of case studies of societies in the distant past to show how they were exposed to all manner of environmental hazards from developing peat cover to the fall out from volcanic eruption. Strat Halliday shows the antiquity of settlement on the uplands, demonstrating, like Whittington, how ancient was the disafforestation of much of the land. The drift of much recent archaeological study has been to raise a question about ancient Celtic society akin to that raised about pre-colonial Australia:

> Those who would see the aboriginals as a noble savage, better attuned than white Australians to the needs and moods of the environment, must reckon with the possibility that the aboriginals left an impoverished ecosystem behind them. (Bolton 1981, p. 10).

As was observed in discussion at the conference, we would have a much better idea of the scale of early human impact on the environment if we could be clearer about early demographic history. Is it thinkable in Scotland, as it is thinkable in England that the Iron Age population was as large or larger than mediaeval population? At least one distinguished archaeological scholar is prepared to affirm that 'there is now some agreement that by the second century AD Britain was experiencing a peak of population expansion, probably of the order of 5 million, which was preceded by a period of rapid growth beginning in the first millenium BC' (Cunliffe 1985). Such a perspective transforms our ideas of the relative importance of the Iron Age.

Environmental history is often a matter of interpreting difficult, fragmentary and complex sources: at our present stage of understanding of the techniques and evidence available, different emphases and interpretations are to be expected. They are also to be welcomed. The two chapters on woodland exploitation differ; the first, on a wide canvas, emphasising the damage done to natural woodland cover before modern capitalist exploitation, which in some cases reversed the trend by giving a value to timber; and the second, a local study, emphasising the conservation ethic of a traditional Highland clan and the dire effects of its rupture. There is a debate here that needs to be refined and extended by further research, in which the input of historical botany will undoubtedly contribute a great deal.

The remaining chapters concentrate on different faunal groups. Alexander Mather grasps the nettle of the impact of sheep on the Highlands, raising the question as to how far they deserve the blame that has been heaped upon them since the later nineteenth century for degrading the moors. He concludes that there is some evidence for this, but less than commonly assumed. John Smith traces the great increase in red deer population since the eighteenth century from a range of quantitative and qualitative evidence. These two chapters together focus attention on the scope for historical research on the rapidly changing upland environment since human population began to shrink in 1841 after a century in which it had reached unprecedented heights. Recent work on changes in grouse and predator kills in the last hundred years is worth drawing attention to here (Hudson 1992).

David Summers uses the excellent and lengthy series of salmon-catch figures, which go back well into the nineteenth century, to argue that changes at sea have been more important than changes on the land in explaining variation. Alasdair Roberts, in the only chapter not presented as a paper to the conference, raises the intriguing possibility that midges have only recently become a plague to people in the Highlands. No chapter raises more acutely the problems of what is appropriate evidence or possible explanation in environmental history, or is more suggestive of the possibility that everyday natural phenomena, that we all take as unchanging given facts, may not always have been the same, or had the same interaction with people.

The Editor finally wishes to thank the sponsors of the conference for their support, and in particular Scottish Natural Heritage for a generous subvention towards publishing the book. Robert Lambert kindly compiled the index at very short notice. The enterprise could not have come about without the patient response of the contributors to my askings and proddings, and without the enthusiasm and hard work of Jill Dick of the Scottish Cultural Press in bringing it to fruition.

Bibliography

Allen D E 1976. *The Naturalist in Britain: A Social History.* London

Anderson D, Grove R (eds.) 1987. *Conservation in Africa, People, Policies and Practice.* Cambridge

Bachell A (ed.) 1991. *Highland Landuse: Four Historical and Conservation Perspectives* NCCS, Inverness

Bechman R 1984. *Des Arbres et des Hommes: La Forêt au Moyen-Age* (Paris); transl.1990 (rather poorly): *Trees and Man: Forests in the Middle Ages.* New York

Birks H H 1972. Radio-carbon dated pollen diagrams from Loch Maree. *New Phytologist* :71

Birks H J B et.al. 1988. *The Cultural Landscape - Past, Present and Future.* Cambridge

Bolton G 1981. *Spoils and Spoilers; Australians make their Environment, 1788-1980.* Sydney

Brindlecombe P 1987. *The Big Smoke: a history of air pollution in London since medieval Times.* London

Coates P A 1991. *The Trans-Alaska Pipeline Controversy: Technology, Conservation and the Frontier.* Bethlehem

Cosgrove D 1984. *Social Formation and Symbolic Landscape*. London

Cronan W 1985. *Changes in the Land: Indians, Colonists and the Ecology of New England*. New York

Cronan W 1991. *Nature's Metropolis: Chicago and the Great West, 1848-1938*. New York

Crosby A W 1986. *Ecological Imperialism: the Biological Expansion of Europe 900-1900*. Cambridge

Cunliffe B W 1985. Man and landscape in Britain, 6000BC-AD400. In: Woodell S R J (ed.) *The English Landscape: Past, Present and Future*. Oxford

Dean W 1987. *Brazil and the Struggle for Rubber: a Study in Environmental History* Cambridge

Dickson J H 1993. Scottish woodlands: their ancient past and precarious future. *Botanical Journal of Scotland* 26.

Duncan C A M 1991. On identifying a sound environmental ethic in history: prolegomena to any future environmental history. *Environmental History Review* 15(2): 9

Edwards K J, forthcoming. *Scotland: Environment and Archaeology 8000BC-1000AD*

Frome M 1992. *Regreening the National Parks*. Tucson

Gadgil M, Guha R 1992. *This Fissured Land: an Ecological History of India*. Berkeley

Glacken C J 1967. *Traces on the Rhodian Shore: Nature and Culture in Western Thought from Ancient Times to the End of the Eighteenth Century*. Berkeley

Grove R 1992. Origins of Western environmentalism. *Scientific American* 267(1): 42-46.

Guha R 1990. *The Unquiet Woods: Ecological Change and Peasant Resistance in the Himalya*. Berkeley

Harvie-Brown J A 1879. *The Capercaillie in Scotland*. Edinburgh

Harvie-Brown J A 1881. *The History of the Squirrel in Great Britain*. Edinburgh

Harvie-Brown J A 1892. The Great Spotted Woodpecker (*Picus major* L.) in Scotland. *Annals of Scottish Natural History* 1: 4-17

Hoskings W G 1965. *The Making of the England Landscape*. London

Hou W 1990. The environmental crisis in China and the case for environmental history studies. *Environmental History Review* 14(1-2): 151-58

La Frenière G F 1980. Rousseau and the European roots of environmentalism. *Environmental History Review* 15: 41-72

Lines W 1991. *Taming of the Great South Land: a History of the Conquest of Nature in Australia*. Sydney

MacKenzie J M 1900. *Imperialism and the Natural World*. Manchester

Macinnes L, Wickham-Jones C R 1992. *All Things Natural: Archaeology and the Green Debate*. Oxford

Meinig D W 1962. *On the Margins of the Good Earch: the South Australian Wheat Frontier 1869-1884*. Chicago

Merchant C 1989. *Ecological Revolutions: Nature, Gender and Science in New England*. Chapel Hill

Nairne D 1891. Notes on Highland woods, ancient and modern. *Transactions of the Gaelic Society of Inverness* 17

Nash R 1973. *Wilderness and the American Mind*. New Haven

Oelschlaeger M 1991. *The Idea of Wilderness from Prehistory to the Age of Ecology*. Yale

Olwig K 1984. *Nature's Ideological Landscape*. London

Passmore J 1980. *Man's Responsibility for Nature*. 2nd edn. London

Pepper D 1984. *The Roots of Modern Environmentalism*. London

Price R J 1983. Scotland's Environment During the Last 30,000 Years. Edinburgh

Rackham O 1980. *Ancient Woodland: its History, Vegetation and Uses in England*. London

Rackham O 1986. *The History of the Countryside*. London

Rawat A S (ed.) 1991. *History of Forestry in India*. New Delhi

Ritchie J 1920. *The Influence of Man on Animal Life in Scotland*. Cambridge

Sheail J 1976. *Nature in Trust: the History of Nature Conservation in Britain*. Glasgow

Sheail J 1981. *Rural Conservation in Inter-war Britain*. Oxford

Sheail J 1985. *Pesticides and Nature Conservation: the British Experience, 1950-1975*. Oxford

Sheail J 1987. *Seventy-five years in Ecology: the British Ecological Society*. Oxford

Silver T 1990. *A New Face on the Countryside: Indians, Colonists and Slaves in South Atlantic Forests, 1500-1800*. Cambridge

Simmonds I, Tooley M (eds.) 1981. *The Environment in British Pre-history*. London

Smout T C 1990. The Highlands and the roots of green consciousness, 1750-1990. *Proceedings of the British Academy* 76: 237-63

Thomas H 1983. *Man and the Natural World; a History of the Modern Sensibility*. London

Tipping R 1993. A "History of the Scottish Forests" revisited. *Reforesting Scotland* 8: 16-21; 9: 18-21

White L 1967. The historical roots of our ecologic crisis. *Science* 155 (March 10): 1203-07.

Whitelock D 1985. *Conquest to Conservation: History of Human Impact on the South Australian Environment*. Adelaide

Williams M 1974. *The Making of the South Australian Landscape*. London

Williams M 1989. *Americans and their Forests: a Historical Geography*. Cambridge

Williams R 1973. *The Country and the City*. London

Worster D 1977. *Nature's Economy: a History of Ecological Ideas*. Cambridge

Worster D (ed.) 1988. *The Ends of the Earth*. Cambridge

SETTING THE SCENE
An Overview of Climatic Change

J John Lowe

Introduction

Scotland lies in one of the most sensitive areas of the world in relation to climatic instability—the north east Atlantic and adjacent mainland. People often jest about the unpredictability and constant flux of the weather in Scotland today: the jest could also be couched justifiably in terms of its climate when viewed over a geological timescale. All the available evidence points to a long history of quite major and often very dramatic climatic changes.

The oceanic and atmospheric mechanisms that we recognise as important in the North Atlantic region today—deep water formation, ocean upwelling, North Atlantic Polar Front, 'Gulf Stream', Jet Stream—are subject to many influences, predominant among which is external ('Astronomical') forcing. Over the long term and at the global scale, variations in net receipt of radiation and in the way the radiation flux is distributed over the surface of the earth ultimately call the tune of climatic change. However, this tune is modulated by a complex chain of internal ('feedback') mechanisms (e.g. the volume and state of flux of glacier ice, ocean salinity and circulation patterns, atmospheric gas exchange mechanisms, global sea level, and volcanic activity) so that the pattern of climatic changes are both temporally and spatially complex.

Although the detailed mechanisms of climatic change are still imperfectly understood, significant progress has been made within the last decade in identifying some of the key processes, and it is anticipated that further clarification is just around the corner. Three recent developments have brought about this optimistic situation. The first is the growing army of scientists encouraged to research into climate history and climatic mechanisms, partly because of public anxieties over 'global warming'. The second is the increased collaboration between scientists of varied training and skills (physicists, chemists, geologists, climatologists, etc.) through major international programmes (sponsored, for example, by NATO, the UN, the WMO, the EC). This has been essential to develop the expertise and resources required to model the climate system adequately at the global scale. The third has been major technical developments in aspects of geological research, especially in recovering high quality cores from the ocean floors and the polar ice caps. One of the most important results of this new 'high tech' geological research has been the discovery of just how unstable the world's climate has been.

This chapter sets out to present some of this background, to illustrate the scale of natural climatic variations and Scotland's vulnerable position within the global scheme. An appreciation of this wide perspective provides: (a) the backcloth against which to measure the relationships between climate and human history, a topic which is addressed in other chapters; (b) an essential context for conservation and land management efforts; and (c) vital components of any predictive model of future climatic changes.

Four themes will be used to illustrate the rates of environmental change discernible in the geological record: (i) switching from glacial to interglacial mode; (ii) movements of the North Atlantic Polar Front; (iii) the North Atlantic 'regulator'; and (iv) instability during warm periods. The nature of the evidence will be briefly introduced and some of the major implications of the evidence will be defined. The chapter closes with a summary of the most recent development in the field, the 'flickering switch' hypothesis, which has made an enormous impact on the scientific community, and which has a great bearing on the debate over future climatic change.

Switching from glacial to interglacial mode

The world we inhabit today is a relatively warm one, viewed from the perspective of the last million years or so. The present global climatic regime extends back only about 10,000 years. On average, the earth has experienced colder conditions than now during much of its history. The evidence for this can be found, inter alia, in the records of marine plankton that have accumulated in parts of the deep oceans over the past few million years. They provide two basic types of information from which climatic inferences can be deduced. The first is *biological* information, based on recognising particular assemblages of plankton (diatoms or foraminifera, for example) or individual species that indicate specific water temperature conditions. The second is *chemical* or, more precisely, *isotopic* information.

Micro-organisms within the ocean water column secrete their skeletons or shells from the gaseous and dissolved components of sea water. In doing so, they take up oxygen, which consists mainly of two isotopes, the heavier ^{18}O and the lighter ^{16}O. The ratio between these two isotopes in sea water is dependent upon the combined effects of changes in sea water temperature and also the contemporaneous volume of global ice, since growth of the ice sheets leads to enrichment of the $^{18}O:^{16}O$ ratio in sea water, and vice versa. The analysis of the isotopic records of micro-organisms that inhabited the near-surface layers of the ocean column in particular, provides a record of past variations in sea-water temperature (Ruddiman et al. 1986). Records of the oxygen isotope composition of sea water have been obtained from sediments that have accumulated continuously over the last 3 million years or

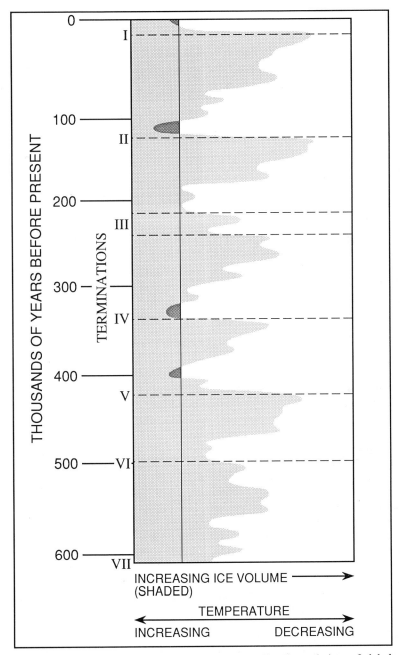

Fig 1.1: The volume of the earth's ice sheets and (indirectly) variations of global climate for the last 600,000 years as deduced from isotopic studies of sea-floor sediments (after Broecker and Denton 1990a)

more (Shackleton et al. 1984). Further details on the methods and principles can be found in Lowe and Walker (1984), Bradley (1985), Sutcliffe (1985), Bell and Walker (1992), Dawson (1992) and Williams et al. (1993).

Figure 1.1 represents a typical oxygen isotope 'curve' for the last 600,000 years or so. The data are interpreted in terms of the volume of global glacier ice—increasing ice volume towards the right. This curve reflects indirectly changing global climate, with increasing warmth to the left. The isotopic data can be presented in a variety of different ways, and a large number of records of varying resolution have been obtained from the floors of the Atlantic, Pacific, and Indian Oceans. The most continuous and detailed records, however, all show some common elements and Fig. 1.1 serves to illustrate some of these.

The curve clearly indicates a cyclic pattern of climatic change. From many other types of geological evidence (see references above) it is known that this represents a shift in conditions between an 'interglacial mode', with ice sheets reduced to a volume comparable with those existing today, and a 'glacial mode', with greatly expanded ice sheets and an extension of the arctic-tundra zone (Lowe and Walker 1984). As Fig. 1.1 suggests, this appears to have followed a regular rhythm, which suggests some recurrent forcing mechanism. The periodicity recorded in the oxygen isotope traces corresponds very closely to the calculated periodicity of net global radiation receipt, which varies over time because of changes in the degree of axial tilt of the earth and in the configuration of the earth's orbit (Imbrie and Imbrie 1979). It is therefore widely accepted that these long-term climatic cycles are primarily driven by such 'Astronomical' variations.

The oxygen isotope record, when examined in detail, suggests a number of other important characteristics of recent global climatic history. First, if the record is taken at face value, the warm periods appear to have commenced abruptly, promoting colossal environmental shifts within a few hundred years. It has been suggested that changes of up to 10°C within two decades have occurred (Johnsen et al. 1992; Taylor et al. 1993). Put another way, glacial epochs terminated abruptly, and specialists in this field recognise a series of distinct 'terminations', numbered I to VII on Fig. 1.1, in the record for the last 600,000 years. On the other hand, periods of cooling appear to have been much more gradual, as can be seen from the much gentler gradients on the cooling limbs of the curve in Fig. 1.1. To interpret these variations directly as a *climatic curve* may be a little misleading, however, since it may be much easier to melt large volumes of glacier ice than to generate them.

A vertical line has been drawn down through the diagram from the point on the curve representing the present day. This may give at least a general indication of those times in the past when temperatures were about as warm as those of today (areas more heavily shaded to the left of the line). Assuming this approach to have some validity, one is struck by the few times when this appears to have been the case, and how short-lived the phases of 'interglacial mode' have been. They appear to have endured for only about 10,000 to 12,000 years, whereas the cold periods seem to have lasted perhaps six to seven times longer. The evidence therefore suggests that we live in an unusually warm period, when viewed against the geological timescale, and one which, in theory, may have run its course. It is on this basis that some scientists refer to the present warm period as an 'interglacial'; that is, a return to glacial conditions is considered inevitable, though the timing is uncertain. This point will be discussed further in the final section of this chapter.

It is likely, therefore, that on average, the climatic conditions of Scotland have been colder than now during the past million years, and the conditions we enjoy today (bleak though they may sometimes appear!) are unusually mild. It is difficult to judge what the 'average' conditions may have been, and what kind of environment and landscape developed as a consequence. We do know, however, that at times of extreme cold, Scotland was subjected to intense ice-sheet glaciation on several occasions, though we only have clear evidence for the pattern and timing of the most recent phase, which terminated approximately 14,000 to 13,000 years ago (Sissons 1967, 1976; Sutherland 1984; Bowen et al. 1986).

An interesting perspective on global climate change has emerged from recent attempts to model sea surface temperatures during the last maximum of ice sheet extension, estimated to around 18,000 years ago, which have in turn been compared with present-day conditions (Fig. 1.2). A group of scientists collaborated under a major, international research programme, termed CLIMAP (Climate: Long-Range Investigation Mapping and Prediction) to compile the evidence for sea-surface temperatures based on geological evidence obtained from many marine cores (CLIMAP Members 1981; Ruddiman and McIntyre 1981). The result is illustrated in Fig. 1.2 (top). Inspection of this figure, and comparison with present-day isotherms (bottom diagram) shows that the greatest differences in sea-surface temperatures between 18,000 years ago and the present day occurred in the north east Atlantic sector. The British Isles, therefore, lie adjacent to the world's most sensitive ocean surface, one that, on at least one occasion in the recent geological past, has experienced shifts of temperature of up to 12°C.

Movements of the 'North Atlantic Polar Front'

At the present time there is a distinct oceanic boundary in the North Atlantic which separates cold, sub-arctic water to the north from more temperate waters to the south. This is termed the 'Oceanic Polar Front' and it presently lies just to the south of Iceland, at approximately the limit of iceberg survival. It generates an active, atmospheric zone, along which frontal systems are steered, and this is termed the 'Atmospheric Polar Front'. The position of the Oceanic Polar Front therefore marks an important boundary between weather systems.

Modelling of ocean surface temperatures for different times, using techniques similar in some respects to those adopted by CLIMAP, have demonstrated that the Oceanic Polar Front has shifted position quite dramatically (Fig. 1.3). At the time of the last glacial maximum, it was

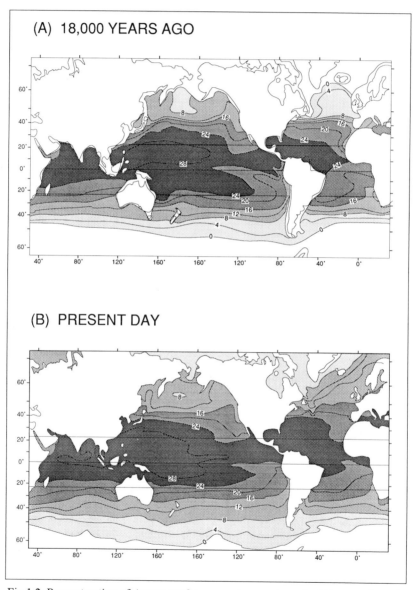

Fig 1.2: Reconstruction of August surface ocean temperatures for (A) approximately 18,000 BP compared with (B) modern sea surface isotherms (based on CLIMAP Project Members, 1981 and Ruddiman and McIntyre 1981)

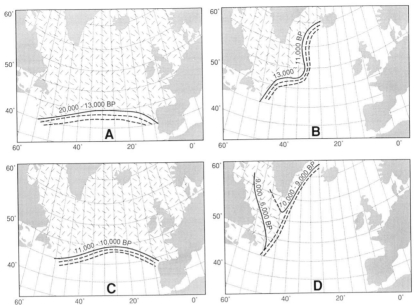

Fig 1.3: Changes in the position of the North Atlantic Oceanic Polar Front from approximately 20,000-9,000BP (after Ruddiman and McIntyre 1981)

situated off northern Portugal at around latitude 40°N (Fig. 1.3a) and cold surface waters lay to the west of the British Isles (Ruddiman and McIntyre 1981). By 13,000 years ago, however, the Polar Front had migrated north to the vicinity of Iceland (Fig. 1.3b) to allow temperate waters to flow around the coastline of northern Europe, thereby accelerating the melting of the ice sheets which were already in decline. These shifts in the position of the North Atlantic Polar Front are the regional expression or consequence of overall changes in North Atlantic circulation.

The consequences for the British Isles of the northward migration of the Polar Front were dramatic. Prior to 13,000BP, most of the British Isles was covered by an ice sheet and locked in continuous sea ice. The prevailing climate was cold continental, with an average summer temperature below 10°C and winter temperatures as cold as -20 to -25°C (Atkinson et al. 1987). Quite suddenly, however, at about or shortly after 13,000BP, and consequent upon the northward migration of the Polar Front, summer temperatures warmed to average about 17°C while average winter temperatures were in the range 0-1°C. Clearly, the position of the Polar Front determines the weather experienced by the British Isles, in large part because it in turn is linked to the path of the Gulf Stream. A southward migration of the Polar Front also means that the Gulf Stream is deflected south, away from the British Isles, though which of these developments leads the other is not possible to tell. It is likely that they are inter-dependent expressions of changes in North Atlantic circulation.

About 11,000BP the Polar Front moved south again, to reach a maximum southerly position off south-west Ireland (Fig. 1.3c), bringing again a climate of arctic severity to much of Europe. The cold spell was sudden and short-lived. It has been estimated that the rate of southward migration of polar waters was somewhere of the order of 5km a year (Bard et al. 1987), but by shortly after 10,000 years ago the Polar Front had migrated northwards again to lie to the north of Iceland (Fig. 1.3d), possibly indicating milder climatic conditions in the North Atlantic sector than today (Ruddiman et al. 1977; Ruddiman and McIntyre 1981).

The period of cold between approximately 11,000 and 10,000BP is termed the Younger Dryas Stadial in Europe and the Loch Lomond Stadial in Britain. Although short-lived, it brought conditions of arctic severity to the British Isles, with average summer temperatures below 10°C and winter temperatures in the range -15 to -20°C (Atkinson et al. 1987). Glaciers occupied many of the Highland valleys of Scotland (Fig. 1.4), with a major icefield in the western Highlands centred on Rannoch Moor, and smaller icefields on Mull and the Isle of Skye (Gray and Lowe 1977; Ballantyne 1984; Sutherland 1984; Thorp 1986; Lowe and Walker 1986; Walker et al. 1988; Ballantyne 1989). Shortly after 10,000BP most of this ice had disappeared, as the British Isles were once again enveloped in the warm waters of the Gulf Stream (Fig. 1.3d).

The Younger Dryas event has intrigued scientists for many years. It cannot be explained by the theory of 'Astronomical' variations, as it is too short-lived and, in fact, occurred during a period of radiation maximum. It seems to have been an interruption in a transition from the last glacial period to the present interglacial. Some have therefore referred to the preceding warm phase, between 13,000 and 11,000BP, as a 'false start' to the present interglacial.

The importance of the event is two-fold. Firstly, it indicates just how rapidly the climate can switch between quite extreme states—what has been described by several leading scientists as a 'flip' between interglacial to glacial mode and back again. When one considers the devastating effect the Younger Dryas cold snap had on the Scottish environment, any evidence to show that it could be a recurrent phenomenon would be sobering indeed. Secondly, it shows that factors other than 'Astronomical' variations can bring about major climatic changes. Most important in this respect are the combined roles of ice melting and oceanic circulation, a topic which is introduced next.

The North Atlantic 'Regulator'

Recent accounts of climatic change have emphasised the role of ocean circulation, and especially the operation of what has become known as the 'Oceanic Conveyor Belt' (Fig. 1.5). This is a simplified model of a global ocean circulation system driven by changes in temperature and salinity. Surface waters in equatorial and tropical regions, initially warm and of low salinity, move northwards into the North Atlantic where they become cold, dense and saline. This water mass then sinks and returns as deep water southwards and around the southern tip of Africa, whereafter it spreads into the Indian and Pacific Oceans. It then warms and rises and is driven westwards again as a surface current to reconnect with Atlantic surface waters. So the circulation is complete, and the system is maintained by heat exchange and the density gradients set up by salinity differences.

There is evidence to suggest that this conveyor system was 'switched off' during glacial episodes, as fossil evidence indicates periodic reduced oxygenation and current flow in deep Atlantic waters (Broecker and Denton 1990a, 1990b). It appears that, during cold episodes, the North Atlantic vertical circulation was attenuated, reducing heat transfer into the northern waters which either led to, or was consequent upon, the expansion of glaciers in adjacent areas.

It is not really known what mechanism led to the regular switching off of the conveyor in the North Atlantic, though changes in salinity gradients are obviously suspected. However, an extension of this idea has led to an

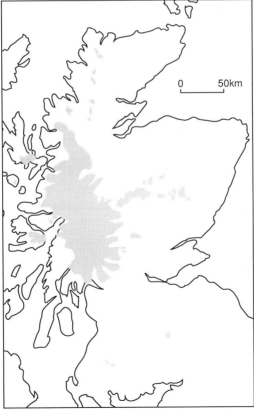

Fig 1.4: Approximate maximum extent of glacier ice on the Scottish mainland and Inner Hebrides during the Younger Dryas event (approx. 11,000-10,000BP)

attractively simple explanation for the Younger Dryas event. As the main ice sheets melted back at the end of the last glacial episode, huge volumes of freshwater were delivered into the North Atlantic. Especially important here was the release of waters ponded against the retreating margin of the North American ice sheet, leading to the catastrophic drainage of water along the St Lawrence (Broecker et al. 1989; Teller 1990). It has been proposed that this led to a surface layer of water that was not only cold, but also of low salinity, which effectively put a 'lid' on the North Atlantic limb of the conveyor, thereby blocking the northward transfer of heat leading to further cooling and the expansion of glaciers.

Whether these mechanisms operated in quite this way is a matter of current debate, since some recent research does not fully support the sequence of events proposed (Fairbanks 1989). The importance of this hypothesis, however, lies in focusing our attention on the inter-connections between different parts of the earth system. The melting of the huge ice sheets must have had significant physical effects upon the oceans, which in turn must have modulated their circulation in some way. Equally, of course, the operation of oceanic circulation affects weather systems and the dynamics of the ice sheets. While 'Astronomical' variations may ultimately drive the earth between glacial and interglacial modes, much more abrupt and short-lived climate changes may be triggered by feedback adjustments in the ocean-ice-atmosphere system.

The idea has gradually emerged, therefore, that the ocean conveyor may have acted as a regulator for climate change (Jones 1991) and that the ocean currents may be in a constant state of flux, with minor variations even during warm periods. Indeed Mörner (1984) has argued for a 'pulsating' Gulf Stream while Kellogg (1984) has provided evidence to show that surface waters in the Denmark Strait have been affected almost continuously by short-term oscillations in surface temperature since the disappearance of the last great ice sheets. Even small variations in the mode of operation of the Gulf Stream may have significant effects on the Scottish climate.

Instability during warm periods

What appear to be periods of warm, stable conditions (the interglacials) are themselves subject to climatic variations. Evidence for such variations during the present interglacial have recently been reviewed by Matthews (1992) and a concise summary can be found in Bell and Walker (1992).

A 'climatic optimum' occurred during the early to middle part of the Holocene, and since then cooler and wetter conditions have generally dominated. A particularly cool and wet phase, termed the Little Ice Age, occurred during the fourteenth to eighteenth centuries AD, when average annual temperatures were some 2-3°C colder than those of the Climatic Optimum and 1-3°C colder than those of the present day (Lamb 1977). There seems little doubt that agricultural yields were significantly affected, and that this at least contributed to the economic and social difficulties experienced in many districts during this period (Le Roy Ladurie 1972; Lamb 1977).

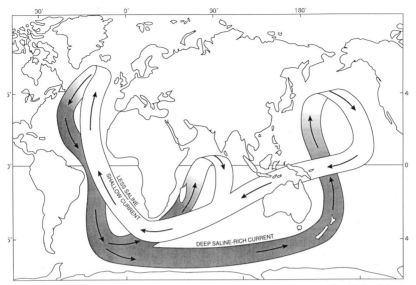

Fig 1.5: Generalised scheme of the global 'ocean conveyor system' of salinity-driven ocean circulation

The extent to which Scotland was affected by climatic variations during the earlier (prehistoric) stages of the Holocene is currently being investigated by a number of research teams. One principal line of evidence is the analysis of fossil pine trees which are abundant throughout many parts of the Scottish Highlands, exposed in the extensive peat haggs that are characteristic of upland plateaux. Pine appears to have been much more prolific and widespread in the country during periods of drier, warmer weather, while peat accumulation was accelerated during times of colder and wetter conditions (Bridge et al. 1990). A particularly marked reduction in the distribution of pine occurred around 4,000 years ago and this is thought, at least in part, to reflect deteriorating climatic conditions. Evidence obtained from peat sequences in Sutherland suggests rapid migrations in the northern treeline for pine, which are also thought to be the result of climatic control (Gear and Huntley 1991). Bridge et al. (1990) have reviewed the evidence from Scotland for the incidence of pine fossils and, on the basis of this, have suggested that particularly wet periods occurred at around 5,700-5,250, 3,800-3,500 and immediately post-3250 years ago (Fig. 1.6).

More recently a new dimension has been added to the interpretation of these records by the discovery of volcanic ash layers (tephra) in Scottish peats. The ash originates from Icelandic volcanic centres and at least one of the main ash bands coincides with the evidence for the southward shift of pine in Scotland about 4,000 years ago. It has therefore been suggested that the demise of pine was caused either by acid pollution resulting from the volcanic ash fall or by a volcanically-induced climatic perturbation (Blackford et al. 1992).

It is clear, therefore, that climate is unstable even during interglacial stages. For the Scottish environment, with its extreme oceanic position, that must mean that periods of increased wetness and storminess alternated with more clement periods. The tasks that still face us are to unravel this climatic history in full and to quantify the nature and effects of the climatic shifts.

The information that has accumulated for the climatic history of the present interglacial has, to an extent, influenced interpretations of earlier interglacial records. Because the present interglacial has been generally warm for 10,000 years, and subject to only comparatively minor climatic oscillations, this has been considered to be the norm for interglacial stages. That view has now been challenged, with the publication of a detailed record of climatic variations represented in ice cores from Greenland (GRIP Project Members 1993). This evidence indicates that the last interglacial (dated approximately to between 125,000 and 115,000 years ago) was characterised by a series of short-lived but severe cold episodes, although the glacial evidence also suggests that the maximum warmth of the last interglacial was greater than that of the present interglacial. This indicates that the long-lasting, generally warm conditions of the present interglacial may be an exceptional event within recent geological history. The implications of this are far-reaching, as indeed are other aspects of the ice-core records, which are discussed further in the following section.

The 'flickering switch' hypothesis

Ice cores are remarkable archives of past environment variations. As snow accumulates on ice-sheet surfaces, it traps dust (some derived from volcanic activity) and air bubbles. The snow is compacted to form a layer of ice and

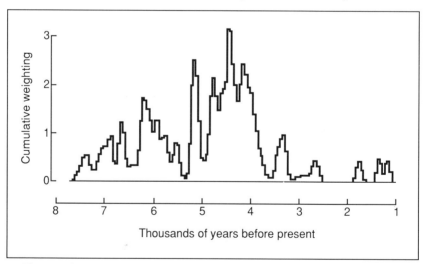

Fig 1.6: Histogram of frequency of radiocarbon-dated pine stumps from Scotland (n=96) based on Bridge et al. 1989. Wet climatic periods are thought to have caused the troughs represented in the histogram at c5700-5250, 3800-3500, and post-3250BP

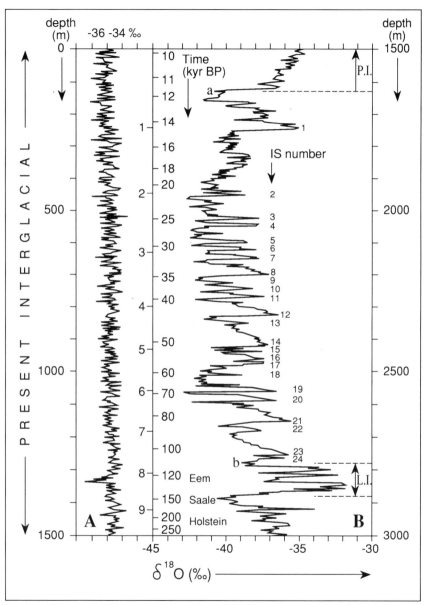

Fig 1.7: Oxygen isotope curve from the GRIP ice core, Greenland, for the past 250,000 years (after Dansgaard et al. 1993). Diagram A (left) represents present interglacial, present-day to 10,000 years ago. Diagram B (main figure) represents the period 10,000 to 250,000 years ago. The measures are of the ratio between ^{18}O and ^{16}O isotopes. Sudden 'interstadial' warmings are numbered 1-24. LI = Last Interglacial; PI = Present Interglacial

annual layers are preserved to form an incremental series. Thus annual layers can be counted down from the surface and can also be recognised through a variety of physical measures. These archives have been investigated in both the Antarctic and Greenland ice sheets, providing environmental records of over 200,000 years time span (see Bradley 1985; Oeschger and Langway 1989; Williams et al. 1993). The environmental record is derived from measures of trapped gas bubbles, the water of which the ice is composed, and trapped impurities such as dust. The gas, for example, preserves a record of atmospheric composition, while oxygen isotope ratios in the water component are related to climatic conditions. GRIP (Greenland Ice-core Project) is an international collaboration programme dedicated to the analysis of deep ice cores obtained from central Greenland. The records obtained from this project have really proved quite remarkable, since they show a large number of abrupt climatic shifts, most of which have not been detected previously by other geological methods. The climate record reported by the GRIP research is illustrated in Fig. 1.7 (Dansgaard et al. 1993). It suggests a number of short-lived and abrupt warmings (numbered 1 to 24 in Fig. 1.7) that interrupt the general cold of the last glacial stage (115,000 to *ca.*13,000 years ago). The implication is that the Earth's climate system can flip quite suddenly between stable states. There is nothing gradual about climate change, according to these ice core records, but rather a 'flickering switch' operates—the analogue is the sudden effect of switching on and off a light (Taylor et al. 1993).

When these records were first published, scientists took comfort in the thought that these very dramatic climatic 'flips', if they can be read as such at face value, occurred during a cold, glacial stage. During such periods, instability is to be expected because of the feedback effects of the changing volume of the ice sheets, changing sea levels, alteration in atmospheric composition, and so on. Thus each 'switch' may be explained by some adjustment in the ice-sea-atmosphere balance, as has been suggested earlier to provide an explanation for the Younger Dryas event. Nevertheless, this is a much higher pulse rate with a stronger signal than had previously been suspected.

Even more intriguing are the suggestions by the GRIP team that rapid shifts in temperature are also possible during interglacial periods (GRIP Project Members 1993). This has effectively removed the sense of security that stemmed from the assumption that the 'flickering switch' does not operate during interglacial periods. This assumption is being increasingly challenged, and the thought has emerged that we live in a very unusual period of quiescence in a volatile climatic system:

> We humans have built a remarkable socio-economic system during perhaps the only time when it could be built, when climate was stable enough to let us develop the agricultural infrastructure required to maintain an advanced society. We don't know why we have been so blessed, but without human intervention, the climate system is capable of stunning variability. If the Earth had an operating manual, the chapter on climate might begin with a caveat that the system has been adjusted at the factory for optimum comfort, so *don't touch the dials.* (White 1993, p. 186)

Bibliography

Atkinson T C, Briffa K R, Coope G R 1987. Seasonal temperatures in Britain during the past 22,000 years, reconstructed using beetle remains. *Nature* 325: 587-92

Ballantyne C K 1984. The Late Devensian periglaciation of upland Scotland. *Quaternary Science Reviews* 3: 311-43

Ballantyne C K 1989. The Loch Lomond readvance on the Isle of Skye, Scotland: glacier reconstruction and palaeoclimatic implications. *Journal of Quaternary Science* 4: 95-108

Bard E, Arnold M, Maurice P, Duprat J, Moyes J, Duplessy J-C 1987. Retreat velocity of the North Atlantic polar front during the last deglaciation determined by 14C accelerator mass spectrometry. *Nature* 328: 791-94

Bell M, Walker M J C 1992. *Late Quaternary Environmental Change: Physical and Human Perspectives*. Longman, Harlow

Blackford J J, Edwards K J, Dugmore A J, Cook G T, Buckland P C 1992. Icelandic volcanic ash and the mid-Holocene Scots pine pollen decline in northern Scotland. *The Holocene* 2: 260-65

Bowen D Q, Rose J, McCabe A M, Sutherland D G. 1986. Correlation of Quaternary glaciations in England, Ireland, Scotland and Wales. *Quaternary Science Reviews* 5: 299-340

Bradley R S 1985. *Quaternary Palaeoclimatology: Methods of Paleoclimatic Reconstruction*. Allen & Unwin, London

Bridge M C, Haggart B A, Lowe J J 1990. The history and palaeoclimatic significance of subfossil remains of *Pinus sylvestris* in blanket peats from Scotland. *Journal of Ecology* 78: 77-99

Broecker W S, Denton G H 1990a. What drives glacial cycles? *Scientific American* 262: 43-51

Broecker W S, Denton G H 1990b. The role of ocean-atmosphere reorganisation in glacial cycles. *Quarternary Science Reviews* 9: 305-41

Broecker W S, Kennett J P, Flowe B P, Teller J T, Trumbo S, Bonani G, Wolfli W 1989. Routing of meltwater from the Laurentide Ice Sheet during the Younger Dryas cold period. *Nature* 341: 318-21

CLIMAP Project Members 1981. Seasonal reconstructions of the earth's surface at the Last Glacial Maximum. *Geological Society of America Map and Chart Series* MC-36: 1-18 and maps

Dansgaard W et al. 1993. Evidence for general instability of past climate from a 250-kyr ice-core record. *Nature* 364: 218-20

Dawson A G 1992. *Ice Age Earth: Late Quaternary Geology and Climate*. Routledge, London

Fairbanks R G 1989. A 17,000-year glacio-eustatic sea level record: influence of glacial melting rates on the Younger Dryas event and deep-sea circulation. *Nature* 342: 637-42

Gear A J, Huntley B 1991. Rapid changes in the range limits of Scots pine 4,000 years ago. *Science* 251: 544-47

Gray J M, Lowe J J 1977. *Studies in the Scottish Lateglacial Environment*. Pergamon, Oxford

GRIP Project Members 1993. Climate instability during the last interglacial period recorded in the GRIP ice core. *Nature* 364: 203-7

Imbrie J, Imbrie K P 1979. *Ice Ages: Solving the Mystery*. Macmillan, London

Johnsen S J et al. 1992. Irregular glacial interstadials recorded in a new Greenland ice core. *Nature* 359: 311-13

Jones G A 1991. A stop-start ocean conveyor. *Nature* 349: 364-65

Kellogg T B 1984. Late-glacial Holocene high-frequency climatic changes in deep-sea cores from the Denmark Strait. In: Mörner A, Karlen W (eds.) *Climatic Changes on a Yearly to Millenial Basis*. Reidel, Dordrecht

Lamb H H 1977. *Climate Present Past and Future*. 2 vols. Methuen, London

Le Roy Ladurie E 1972. *Times of Feast, Times of Famine*. Allen & Unwin, London

Lowe J J, Walker M J C 1984. *Reconstructing Quaternary Environments*. Longman, London

Lowe J J, Walker M J C 1986. Lateglacial and early Flandrian environmental history of the Isle of Mull, Inner Hebrides, Scotland. *Transactions of the Royal Society of Edinburgh: Earth Science* 77: 1-20

McIntyre A et al. 1976. Glacial North Atlantic 18,000 years ago: a CLIMAP reconstruction. *Geological Society of America Memoir* 145: 43-75

Matthews J A 1992. *The Ecology of Recently-Deglaciated Terrain*. Cambridge Studies in Ecology, Cambridge University Press

Mörner N-A 1984. Planetary, solar, atmospheric, hydrospheric and endogene processes as origin of climatic changes on the earth. In: Mörner N-A, Karlen W (eds.) *Climatic Changes on a Yearly to Millennial Basis*. Reidel, Dordrecht

Oeschger H, Langway C C Jr (eds.) 1989. *The Environmental Record in Glaciers and Ice Sheets*. John Wiley, Chichester

Ruddiman W F, McIntyre A 1981. The North Atlantic ocean during the last deglaciation. *Palaeogeography, Palaeoclimatology, Palaeoecology* 35: 145-214

Ruddiman W F, McIntyre A, Shackleton N J 1986. North Atlantic sea-surface temperatures for the last 1.1 million years. In: Summerhayes C P, Shackleton N J (eds.) *North Atlantic Palaeoceanography*. Geological Society of America Special Publication 21: 155-73

Ruddiman W F, Sancetta C D, McIntyre A 1977. Glacial-interglacial response rate of subpolar North Atlantic waters to climatic change: the record in oceanic sediments. *Philosophical Transactions of the Royal Society, London*. B280: 119-42

Shackleton N J et al. 1984. Oxygen isotope calibration of the onset of ice-rafting and history of glaciation in the North Atlantic region. *Nature* 307: 620-23

Sissons J B 1967. *The Evolution of Scotland's Scenery*. Oliver & Boyd, Edinburgh

Sissons J B 1976. *The Geomorphology of the British Isles: Scotland*. Methuen, London

Sutcliffe A J 1985. *On the Track of Ice Age Mammals*. British Museum (Natural History), London

Sutherland D G 1984. The Quaternary deposits and landforms of Scotland and the neighbouring shelves: a review. *Quaternary Science Reviews* 3: 157-254

Taylor K C et al. 1993. The 'flickering switch' of late Pleistocene climate change. *Nature* 361: 432-36

Teller J T 1990. Meltwater and precipitation runoff to the North Atlantic, Arctic, and Gulf of Mexico from the Laurentide ice sheet and adjacent regions during the Younger Dryas. *Paleoceanography* 5: 897-905

Thorp P 1986. A mountain ice field of Loch Lomond Stadial age, western Grampians, Scotland. *Boreas* 15: 83-97

Walker M J C, Ballantyne C K, Lowe J J, Sutherland D G 1988. A reinterpretation of the Lateglacial environmental history of the Isle of Skye, Inner Hebrides, Scotland. *Journal of Quaternary Science* 3: 135-46

White J W C 1993. Don't touch that dial. *Nature* 364: 186

Williams M A J, Dunkerley D L, De Deckker P, Kershaw A P, Stokes T 1993. *Quaternary Environments*. Edward Arnold, London

2

HUMAN IMPACT ON THE PREHISTORIC ENVIRONMENT

Kevin J Edwards

Introduction

This century has seen much research into the environmental history of Scotland (Price 1983). This has provided a context for the human occupation of at least the last 10,000 years (cf. Thoms 1979; Mellars 1987). We now have an excellent knowledge of vegetation history and, by inference, climate and soil histories, which arise largely as a result of the pollen method (Edwards 1973; Walker 1984; Whittington, this volume). In this chapter, the emphasis is switched in order to look at the impact of prehistoric peoples upon their environment (topics 1-3 below), before returning to potential environmental influences upon human communities (topics 3 and 4). This chapter takes the form of a series of case studies with evidence drawn largely from pollen, related sedimentary records and radiocarbon dating. Unless stated otherwise, all dates are expressed as uncorrected radiocarbon (^{14}C) years BP (before present; the conventional method in environmental research) and BC.

1. Mesolithic hunter-gatherers and Neolithic agriculturalists: Kinloch, Rum

The Inner Hebridean island of Rum possesses the oldest known occupation site in Scotland. At Farm Fields, Kinloch, beside Loch Scresort (Figs. 2.1, 2.2), a formerly extensive Mesolithic hunter-gatherer presence is indicated by spreads of lithic materials (flint and bloodstone), charred hazel nut shells, and structures (Wickham-Jones 1990). Dates derived from the Mesolithic archaeological contexts span the period 8590-7570BP (6640-5620BC). Neolithic age features include a charred hazel nut shell dated to 4725±140 BP (2775±140BC), pottery, and ditch and slopewash materials (dated 4260±70 [2310±70BC] and 3945±50BP [1995±50BC]).

Pollen, charcoal and sedimentary records produced from a site 300 m west of the excavations (Fig. 2.3) cover the period 7800±75BP (5850±75BC) to the present day (Hirons and Edwards 1990). They therefore cover the end of the on-site Mesolithic archaeological record and go beyond it into that period

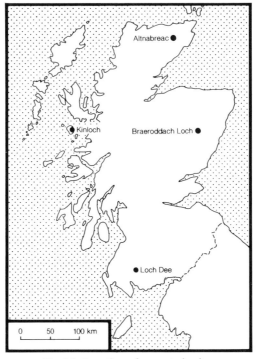

Fig 2.1. Location of case study sites

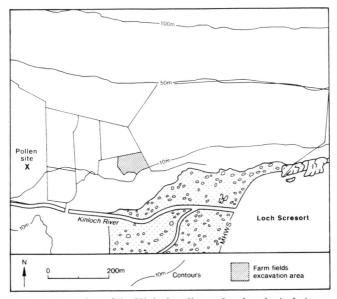

Fig 2.2. Location of the Kinloch pollen and archaeological sites

of Mesolithic time which was not recovered from the excavation. The palaeoenvironmental evidence reveals sharp changes in pollen and charcoal records which would seem to reflect changes in vegetation which may be ascribed to the impacts of hunter-gatherer communities. Alder (*Alnus*) pollen is much reduced in pollen zones KII-b/c and KII-d and hazel (cf. Coryloid) in zone KIIb/c, and these are times of abundant microscopic charcoal. It is not being suggested that fire was being used in woodland clearance—felling by axe may have been taking place at the same time as felled timber was being burnt for cooking and heating purposes. It is even conceivable that felling was part of a woodland management regime to promote hazel, alder and willow (*Salix*) coppice (cf. Göransson 1986). The expansion of alder after the appearance of a major peak in charcoal is paralleled at other sites (Edwards 1990), but it is difficult to separate natural from possible anthropogenic impacts in the early part of the pollen profile. The analysis of inwashed minerogenic particles also suggests that activities led to disturbances in soils and probably vegetation on the slopes overlooking the pollen site.

Cereal-type (Cerealia) pollen appears from about 3950BP (2000BC)—a time around which eroded slopewash materials, perhaps agriculturally-liberated, were being deposited in the eastern segment of the excavation area. The major expansion of grass (Gramineae) pollen in zone KIII-a, however, probably indicates that animal husbandry was of greater significance (or environmental change forced it to become so) than arable to Neolithic agriculturalists in Rum.

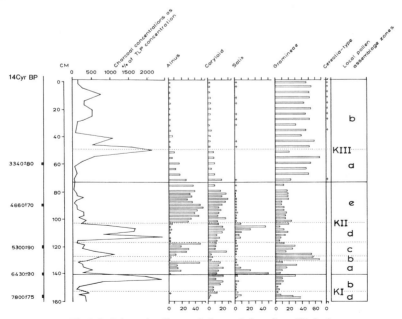

Fig 2.3. Selected pollen and charcoal data from Kinloch

2. Middle Bronze Age and Iron Age agriculturalists: Braeroddach Loch, Aberdeenshire

The small lake site of Braeroddach Loch is located in the Grampian foothills some 44 km west of Aberdeen. Close to the site are located two Neolithic long cairns, five large round cairns and two cists of presumed Bronze Age date, and four field and settlement systems generally assigned to the Iron Age (Fig. 2.4). The site was chosen for study because of the sensitive palaeoenvironmental record (Fig. 2.5) which it was anticipated might be recovered from a small loch site, and the proximity of archaeological monuments (Edwards 1975, 1978; Edwards and Rowntree 1980).

A steepening of the time-depth curve coupled with more minor palaeoecological changes at about 4600BP (2650BC) suggest landscape impacts from Neolithic agriculturalists. More substantial impacts become apparent from a middle Bronze Age date of *ca.* 3065±120BP (1115±120BC) after which woodland pollen goes into decline, cereal pollen makes its first appearance, sedimentary indicators (chemical and magnetic) rise, and radiocarbon dates start to go into reverse. It seems fairly clear that this pattern reflects woodland clearance and cereal cultivation, agriculturally-induced soil erosion (leading to increased inputs of such sedimentary indicators as sodium and magnetic susceptibility), and the inputs of eroded soils containing old carbon into the loch as sediment (thus 'ageing' the radiocarbon dates). The rise in charcoal values may also reflect more intensive land use and could result from burning of felled woodland or domestic activities. The impacts evident at Braeroddach Loch did not come to a (temporary) end until the middle Iron Age, some 2000 years ago.

3. Upland grazing, erosion and the spread of blanket peat: Loch Dee, Galloway Hills

Exposures in blanket peat deposits beside Loch Dee in the Galloway Hills (Fig. 2.6), revealed sand- and silt-rich minerogenic layers within the peat stratigraphy (Fig. 2.7). These were of interest because of the possibility that human impact may have been partly or wholly responsible for the deposition of the mineral layers (cf. Simmons et al. 1975), and for the evidence which such sites may furnish concerning the influence of peat development upon human activity (Edwards et al. 1991).

A 108 cm thick deposit at the study site began to form *ca.* 5340±40BP (3390±40)BC and contained four concentrations of minerogenic material. Prior to the deposition of the first minerogenic layer, relatively homogeneous pollen spectra dominated by oak (*Quercus*), alder and hazel pollen, with an understorey of ferns (Filicales), are indicated. The deposition of the first minerogenic layer in Neolithic times at around 4000BP (2050BC), may be related to small scale woodland disturbance (woodland pollen values fall and there is a small increase in herbaceous pollen taxa).

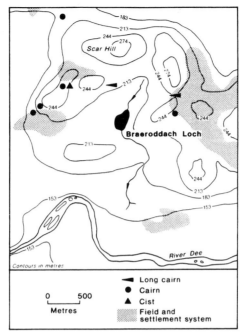

Fig 2.4. Archaeological sites close to Braeroddach Loch

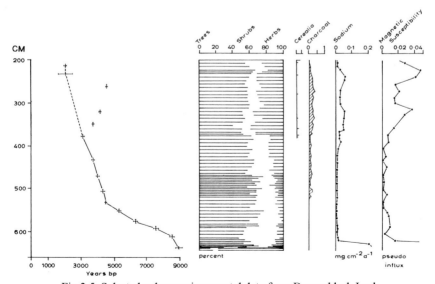

Fig 2.5. Selected palaeoenvironmental data from Braeroddach Loch

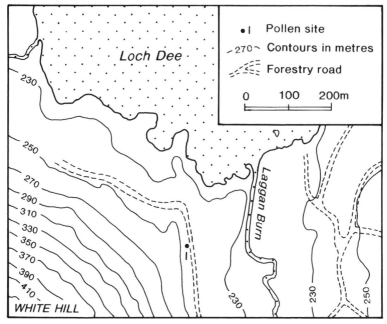

Fig 2.6. Location of Loch Dee study site

More dramatic events seem to occur *ca.* 2600BP (650BC), close to the temporal boundary between the Bronze and Iron Ages, and possibly associated with the formation of minerogenic layers 2 and 3. Microscopic charcoal rises, oak, alder and hazel pollen fall, along with ferns, and there is an increase in the frequencies of birch (*Betula*), rowan type (*Sorbus*), grass, ribwort plantain (*Plantago lanceolata*) and cereal type pollen. The suggestion is of woodland clearance for pasture (and arable in lower-lying areas, where the alder woodland was also probably located), and the increased representation for birch and rowan type may derive from the regeneration of such taxa within or at the edges of cleared areas. The rise in charcoal, once again, is probably anthropogenic in origin.

From this time onwards the pollen diagram is increasingly dominated by grasses, sedges (Cyperaceae), and latterly heather (*Calluna*). There is a fourth minerogenic layer, possibly occurring at around 1760BP (190AD) associated with woodland decline, a rise in charcoal and the presence of cereal type pollen, but the general impression is one of the fuller development of an unwooded moorland landscape—the deposit itself, of course, is testimony to the spread of peat. Thus, a usable, partially wooded landscape, upon which humans in prehistoric and historical times had a passing influence, succumbed to the extension of peat (whether for anthropogenic, climatic or soil-related reasons [cf. Moore 1993]). The Forestry Commission are now doing their best to restore the area to woodland, albeit by the imposition of a drab cloak of non-native sitka spruce.

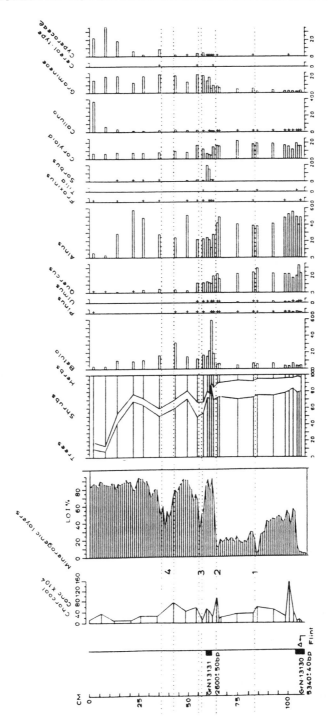

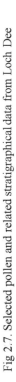

Fig 2.7. Selected pollen and related stratigraphical data from Loch Dee

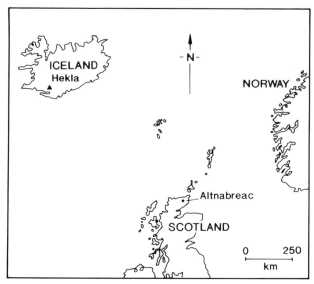

Fig 2.8. Location of the Altnabreac study area in Caithness and the Hekla volcano,
Iceland

4. Volcanic impacts?: Altnabreac, Caithness

The devastating local effects of volcanic eruptions, from lava, pyroclastic
ejecta, fires, floods and gases, are well documented (Sheets and Grayson
1979). In Iceland the Lakigígar eruption of 1783-84 produced the world's
largest historical lava flow and may have led to the deaths of 77 percent of
the livestock and 22 percent of the population of Iceland (Ólafsson 1861;
Gunlaugsson et al. 1984). Its impact, however, was wider and in Caithness,
1783 was spoken of 'as the year of the ashie' and fine volcanic dust was
reported as destroying crops (Geikie 1893). The same eruption was noted by
Benjamin Franklin (1784) as colouring the sunsets over Paris. The actual and
potential impacts of eruptions upon world climate also continue to receive
attention. The archaeologist John Barber has conjectured that the eruption of
Hekla-3, *ca.* 1170 calendar years BC, may even have been implicated in the
possible abandonment of marginal settlement in northern Scotland (cf.
Burgess 1989; Baillie 1989).

At Altnabreac in Caithness (Fig. 2.8), tephra or ash layers consisting of
shards of microscopic glass, have been assigned to the eruption of the
Icelandic volcano Hekla at around 3800BP (1850BC; eruption Hekla-4 [H-4];
Dugmore 1989). The tephra layers at Altnabreac may provide a surrogate for
the environmental effects of other eruptions and it has subsequently been
studied in greater detail (Blackford et al. 1992).

The Altnabreac H-4 ash appears to have been a heavy fall, and glass
shards are present in concentrations sometimes in excess of 1 million shards
per cubic centimetre of peat (Figure 2.9). Preceding the tephra peak, values
of pine (*Pinus*) pollen are nearly 20 percent of the pollen sum. Over the next

1.4 cm of the pollen diagram, pine percentages drop to less than 2 percent, accompanied by increases in the relative proportions of blanket peat taxa (including *Erica* type, Cyperaceae and *Sphagnum*) and a decrease in heather. Hypotheses which may be suggested to explain events at Altnabreac include the possibility that the eruption of Hekla caused a climatic change of sufficient magnitude to alter the hydrological regime of the blanket bog at Altnabreac, and/or that the fallout of tephra had a direct effect by causing acid deposition (from volatiles adsorbed onto tephra particles)—a prehistoric acid rain! The changes in the mire taxa, in particular, could be interpreted as showing a change to wetter bog-surface conditions, which would also lead to a reduction in heather which prefers somewhat drier habitats. The growth of pine may have been inhibited by either increased wetness or toxic fallout; Caithness was already a marginal area for pine, which had reached its most northerly distribution in Scotland shortly before the time of H-4 tephra deposition. Tephra deposition may also have exacerbated the stress which *Pinus* was under as a result of larger scale climatic changes (cf. the British Isles 'pine decline' of *ca.* 2000BC [Bennett 1984]).

The extent to which volcanic activity might have instigated such environmental changes in prehistory remains to be shown. The increasingly frequent identification of tephra layers in Scottish deposits (Bennett et al. 1992; Edwards et al. in press) may well permit a critical examination of archaeologically-inspired hypotheses of settlement change.

Conclusions

The studies presented here cover many different time periods and different locations within Scotland. They represent snap-shots but, in many instances,

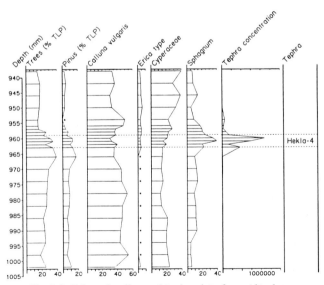

Fig 2.9. Selected pollen and tephra data from Altnabreac

have parallels elsewhere. What is demonstrated is that prehistoric human communities, both hunter-gatherers as well as agriculturalists, have had evident impacts upon their local environments. The scale of impact was often a matter of local geography, but this in no way diminishes the destructive potential of perhaps small populations. Neither is there any reason to suppose that prehistoric peoples were not concerned to manage and preserve their environments: there may have been coppice woodlands at Kinloch, just as managed heathlands are proposed for many areas of Britain in Mesolithic times (e.g. Caseldine and Hutton 1993; Simmons 1993); and it would not have been in farmers' interests to destroy their soils (although we can never be sure of the extent to which farmers were aware of long-term erosion).

In terms of the occupation of an area, however, the environment must be regarded as being capable of strongly influencing the land-use agenda: the removal of plough soils at Kinloch during the Neolithic or at Braeroddach Loch in the Bronze Age may well have influenced the quality or type of subsequent farming activity; did the extension of grassland at Kinloch during the Neolithic represent an effort to foster grazing or was it a response to soil or deterioration? The impact of Icelandic volcanoes may have influenced farming or even the feasibility of settlement in Caithness through acid deposition or climatic change. The human response would have depended upon the fragility of a marginal environment and the technological abilities of a particular prehistoric community (Edwards and Whittington, in press).

It is clear that multidisciplinary exercises are capable of furnishing considerable insights into early human activity, and this will be all the more so as methods are refined. In spite of the uncertainties, the human-environment relationship in prehistory continues to fascinate and many surprises must surely await the investigator.

Bibliography

Baillie M G L. 1989. Hekla 3: how big was it? *Endeavour* New Series 13: 78-81

Bennett K D. 1984. The Post-Glacial history of *Pinus sylvestris* in the British Isles. *Quaternary Science Reviews* 3: 133-56

Bennett K D, Boreham S, Sharp M J, Switsur V R. 1992. Holocene history of environment, vegetation and human settlement on Catta Ness, Lunnasting, Shetland. *Journal of Ecology* 80: 241-73

Blackford J J, Edwards K J, Dugmore A J, Cook G T, Buckland P C 1992. Icelandic volcanic ash and the mid-Holocene Scots pine (*Pinus sylvestris*) pollen decline in northern Scotland. *The Holocene* 2: 260-65.

Burgess C 1989. Volcanoes, catastrophe and global crisis of the late second millennium BC. *Current Archaeology* 10: 325-29

Caseldine C, Hutton J 1993. The development of high moorland on Dartmoor: fire and the influence of Mesolithic activity on vegetation change. In: Chambers F M (ed.) *Climate Change and Human Impact on the Landscape*. Chapman & Hall, London

Dugmore A 1989. Icelandic volcanic ash in Scotland. *Scottish Geographical Magazine* 105: 168-72

Edwards K J 1974. A half-century of pollen-analytical research in Scotland. *Transactions of the Botanical Society of Edinburgh* 42: 211-22

Edwards K J 1975. Aspects of the prehistoric archaeology of the Howe of Cromar. In: Gemmell A M D (ed.) *Quaternary studies in North East Scotland*. Quaternary

Research Association, Department of Geography, University of Aberdeen

Edwards K J 1978. Palaeoenvironmental and archaeological investigations in the Howe of Cromar, Grampian Region, Scotland. Unpublished Ph.D. thesis, University of Aberdeen

Edwards K J 1990. Fire and the Scottish Mesolithic: evidence from microscopic charcoal. In: Vermeersch P M, Van Peer P (eds.) *Contributions to the Mesolithic in Europe*. Leuven University Press, Leuven

Edwards K J, Buckland P C, Blackford J J, Dugmore A J, Sadler J P (in press). The impact of tephra: proximal and distal studies of Icelandic eruptions. *Münchener Geographische Abhandlungen*.

Edwards K J, Hirons K R, Newell P J 1991. The palaeoecological and prehistoric context of minerogenic layers in blanket peat: a study from Loch Dee, southwest Scotland. *The Holocene* 1: 29-39

Edwards K J, Rowntree K M 1980. Radiocarbon and palaeoenvironmental evidence for changing rates of erosion at a Flandrian stage site in Scotland. In: Cullingford R A, Davidson D A, Lewin J (eds.) *Timescales in Geomorphology*. J. Wiley & Son, Chichester and New York:

Edwards K J, Whittington G (in press). Disturbance and regeneration phases in pollen diagrams and their relevance to concepts of marginality. In: Coles G, Mills C, McCormick F (eds.) *On the Edge—Settlement in Marginal Areas*. Oxbow Books, Oxford

Franklin B 1784. Meteorological imaginations and conceptions. *Memoirs of the Literary and Philosophical Society of Manchester* 2: 373-77

Geikie A 1893. *Textbook of Geology* (3rd edn). Macmillan, London

Göransson H 1986. Man and the forests of nemoral broad-leaved trees during the Stone Age. *Striae* 24: 145-52

Gunlaugsson G A, Guðbersson G M, Þorarinsson S, Rafnsson S, Einarsson Þ (eds.) 1984. *Skaftáreldar 1783-1784 Ritgerdir og Heimildir*. Mál og Menning, Reykjavik

Hirons K R, Edwards K J 1990. Pollen and related studies at Kinloch, Isle of Rhum, Scotland, with particular reference to possible early human impacts on vegetation. *New Phytologist* 116: 715-27

Mellars P A 1987. *Excavations on Oronsay: Prehistoric Human Ecology on a Small Island*. Edinburgh University Press, Edinburgh

Ólafsson A 1861. Um búnadarhagi Islendinga. *Skyrslur um Landshagi á Islandi*. vol. 2. Hid, íslenzka bókmenntafélag, Reykjavik

Price R J 1983. *Scotland's Environment During the Last 30,000 Years*. Scottish Academic Press, Edinburgh

Sheets P D, Grayson D K (eds.) 1979. *Volcanic Activity and Human Ecology*. Academic Press, London:

Simmons I G 1993. Vegetation change during the Mesolithic in the British Isles: some amplifications. In: Chambers F M (ed.) *Climate Change and Human Impact on the Landscape*. Chapman & Hall, London

Simmons I G, Atherden M A, Cundill P R, Jones R C 1975. Inorganic layers in soligenous mires of the North Yorkshire Moors. *Journal of Biogeography* 2: 49-56

Thoms L M (ed.) 1979. Early man in the Scottish landscape. *Scottish Archaeological Forum* 9: 1-85

Wickham-Jones C R 1990. *Rhum: Mesolithic and Later sites at Kinloch, Excavations 1984-1986*. : Society of Antiquaries of Scotland Monograph Series No. 7

Acknowledgements

Research at Kinloch and Altnabreac has been supported by The Leverhulme Trust and that at Loch Dee by the Science and Engineering Research Council.

3

POLLEN ANALYSIS AS A TOOL FOR ENVIRONMENTAL HISTORY

Graeme Whittington

Introduction

Today we are continually warned that the way we treat our environment will lead to grief for the generations that follow us. Evidence for that point of view is only too obvious when we survey our landscapes and see the dereliction which has already arisen from past exploitative activities. Perhaps worse is the evidence we do not see, such as the presence of toxic heavy metals in our soils and nitrates in our water reserves. Much of this degradation is laid at the door of science and technology and the cry goes up for us to return to a simpler and cleaner life style. This suggests that our ancestors, especially those of long ago, were scrupulous in their environmental behaviour. Furthermore, it tends to discount changes brought about by natural phenomena which had great environmental repercussions. Such an attitude is very dangerous, as the recent eruptions of Mount St Helens (USA), Nevada del Ruiz (Colombia) and Mount Pinatubo (Philippines) demonstrated.

If we wish to examine change in the past, in terms of type, time and length of occurrence, how might we proceed? Some historians and geographers embrace a chronological method in their work in attempting to achieve answers to the questions posed above; using this approach, they are, however, largely restricted in their researches to the period of written record, which suffers all too often from being a broken time series. Archaeology also gives us information from the past but it can only achieve the illumination of a relatively static situation. What is needed, if we are to chart environmental change over lengthy and continuous periods, is a recording device which has a potential for continuity. There are several of these (Birks and Birks 1980; Bennett et al. 1992) but one which is used most commonly is pollen analysis.

Plate 3.1: Micrographs of pollen grains and spores: they are shown at a magnification of x500. Some are specifically referred to in the text while others exemplify variations that occur. (a) polypody *Polypodium vulgare;* (b) pine *Pinus sylvestris;* (c) field pansy *Viola arvensis;* (d) rhododendron *Rhododendron ponticum;* (e) water lily *Nuphar lutea;* (f) wheat *Triticum aestivum;* (g) two grains of dandelion *Taraxacum officinale;* (h) honeysuckle *Lonicera periclymenum;* (i) amphibious bistort *Persicaria amphibia;* (j) rosebay willowherb *Chamerion angustifolium;* (k) corncockle *Agrostemma githago;* (l) common mallow *Malva sylvestris.*

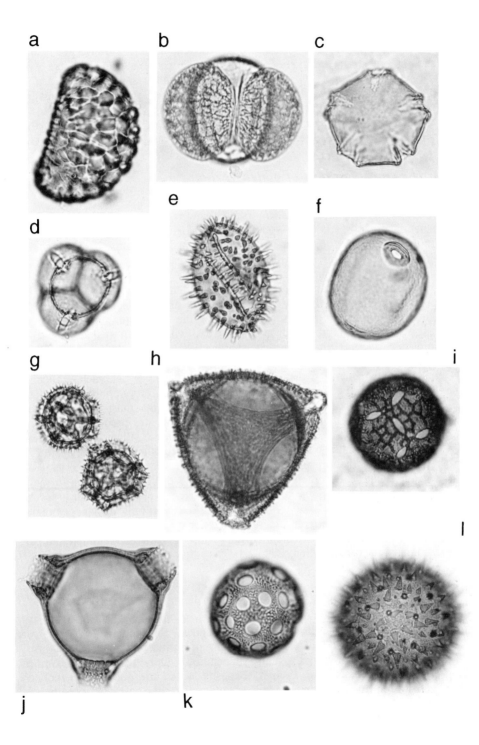

There are three basic factors which provide the foundation for pollen analysis. First, flowering plants produce pollen, while non-flowering plants such as bracken *(Pteridium aquilinum)* produce spores. Secondly, these will survive for long periods if they are deposited on a suitable surface; if a chronological investigation of any length is required, such surfaces must be capable of continuing vertical incrementation. Thirdly, plants are sensitive to environmental change and their response to it will lead to variations in the type of pollen being released into the atmosphere.

Some considerations of pollen grains

Pollen grains are very small (5-100μm and on average about 25μm), and need to be examined under a high-powered microscope, usually at magnifications of times 400-600, although for some identifications, times 1500 is required. They are dispersed from the plants by two main mechanisms; some are carried by the wind and can travel very long distances (Tyldesley 1973), especially those produced by such trees as pine and fir, where air sacs are attached to the main pollen body (Plate 3.1b); others depend upon the activities of a wide variety of insects which visit the plants. This immediately introduces a problem for the pollen analyst. Any pollen spectrum which is revealed by such work will contain pollen from the immediate vicinity and some that has travelled long distances as a result of atmospheric circulation. Thus the pollen analyst speaks of regional and local pollen components and distinguishing between these is extremely difficult. To add to this problem, plants also produce pollen in very variable quantities; for example, grass, heather and hazel are among the most prolific, while potato, violet and rhododendron (Plate 3.1d) are very low producers.

Pollen grains vary very greatly in their appearance (Plate 3.1). They are differentiated from one another by their surface sculpturing, and the apertures which most of them display, and, while some are easily recognised, as with *Nuphar* (Plate 3.1e), others present considerable difficulties in identification (Moore et al 1991). Some are recognisable only at generic or family level, while others, if they are to be exploited to their full, demand extreme attention to minute differences (Whittington and Gordon 1987). For analysts working on human settlement history this is particularly important in distinguishing cereal pollen (Plate 3.1f) from that of other grasses.

The exploitation of pollen and spores

Under the right conditions, pollen can survive for thousands of years in unconsolidated material. For this to happen, the pollen needs to be incorporated into a matrix which is not only anaerobic but which also accumulates steadily and remains undisturbed. Only in that way can a chronological record be assured. Deposits which are suitable for pollen preservation are lacustrine muds, peat and, on a more restricted time basis, palaeosols. All of these also provide innate problems for the pollen analyst.

In addition to the difficulties particular to these sediments, there are others which have to be considered. Perhaps the most important is the fact that pollen and spore preservation, even within the same matrix, can vary greatly (Havinga 1984). Generally speaking spores survive very well. On the other hand, some pollen seems especially prone to early destruction; that of rushes (*Juncus* spp) and yellow flag (*Iris pseudacorus*), for example, are rarely encountered, even though they grow in areas especially suited to pollen preservation. Some pollen grains survive but are so badly decayed or damaged that they can only be placed in an unidentifiable or indeterminate category on pollen diagrams.

Lake muds can suffer from bioturbation which leads to a certain amount of mixing of the deposits of perhaps several years. Slumping of mud from subaqueous slopes can destroy the integrity and thus the chronology of the stratigraphy and the uneven focusing of sediment in certain parts of the lake basin can also cause problems (Davis et al 1984; Edwards and Whittington 1993). In lake sediments, it is necessary to be aware of the problem of meeting material that has been reworked. The deposits in lake basins are partly derived from the erosion, by streams and rain-wash, of material from the land surface. There is a possibility, therefore, that pollen met at a particular level in a core of sediment, which in turn can be allocated to a particular time period, may not be contemporaneous with the other pollen with which it is associated. This is a particular problem, for example, when dealing with sediments laid down in the late glacial period (*ca.* 13-11000BP). At that time, thermophilous trees were absent from the Scottish landscape and yet sediments dated to that period can yield the pollen of such warmth-loving trees as oak, elm and lime (Cundill and Whittington 1983). Such pollen has almost certainly come from the reworking of sediments which had accumulated at a time, many millennia ago, when Scotland's climate had been markedly warmer.

Peat deposits can, like muds, suffer from hiatuses (Barber 1981). In a very dry year a peat surface may not grow, but a more serious problem is cutting for fuel which leads to the removal of centuries of the vegetation record. This is a widespread problem in Scotland where wood for fuel became extremely scarce after the clearance of forests for agriculture from the Neolithic period onwards, and until such times as coal became more accessible to the majority of the population. Furthermore, peat growth can involve many complex variations which the pollen analyst must keep in mind (Clymo 1991).

Palaeosols provide a more restrictive medium for pollen analysis than lake muds or peat. Soils do preserve pollen and spores but pedogenic processes can cause interpretation problems. The movement of water down and up a soil profile can carry pollen and spores with it, as long as the soil has an open enough texture and the pollen and spores are not too large. Root penetration also provides channels down which pollen and spores can infiltrate beyond their correct position in the soil profile. In non-acid soils, pollen tends not to survive very long and earthworm activity mixes up the stratigraphic record (Dimbleby 1985). A further complication can occur in palaeosols in that they frequently reveal high percentages of pollen of

Fig 3.1: A pollen diagram from Northern Fife, covering the vegetation changes over the period 12,670BP until the present. The final column shows local pollen assemblage zones (LPAZ) which suggest successive vegetation association changes.

Asteraceae (e.g dandelions [Plate 3.1g], daisies, thistles). These are likely to be due to the activities of burrowing bees rather than a statement about the local flora (Bottema 1975). It has been suggested that this problem could well be the explanation for the high concentrations of meadowsweet (*Filipendula*) pollen now being found in Bronze Age burials in Scotland, although this is not favoured by those working on this topic. Because of their chemical composition, spores tend to survive very well in soils and will do so even when much pollen, deposited at the same time, has been destroyed. In the analysis of palaeosols, it is quite common to find the spores of ferns in great numbers towards and at the base of the soil profile. It is always necessary to consider whether they are there because the area had a large representation of ferns in its vegetation or if their presence merely reflects their propensity to greater survival. Soils sealed under human constructions (Dimbleby 1985) or under deposits like landslips (Brazier et al 1988) do provide a record of what the vegetation was like over a limited period before the soil burial took place.

Examples of environmental change

To illustrate the features outlined above, some examples of change that have occurred in the Scottish landscape may be selected.

Lacustrine muds in north Fife
In the Ochil Hills of north Fife lies a small rock basin which contains Black Loch. It has over 7m of deposits on its floor and these have been analysed, among other things, for their pollen content (Fig. 3.1). The deposits have also been dated by radiocarbon assay. The pollen analysis allows the demonstration of the enormous changes that have occurred in the landscape since the last major glaciation of Scotland (Whittington et al 1991a). With the removal of the ice from the Fife landscape some 14-13000 years ago, a tundra vegetation was established. It was dominated by grasses (Poaceae), sedges (Cyperaceae), dwarf willow (*Salix herbacea*) and birch (*Betula nana*). As temperatures rose and soil formation developed, more herbaceous plants appeared, such as mugwort (*Artemisia*), sorrel and dock (*Rumex* spp.), meadow rue (*Thalictrum*) and members of the Caryophyllaceae family. After a return to a relatively short cold period (between 11000-10000BP) the climate again started to ameliorate and by 9000BP woodland had begun to be established. Tree birch (*Betula*), oak (*Quercus*), elm (*Ulmus*), hazel (*Corylus avallana*) and alder (*Alnus*) provided a dense forest. This appears to have survived until about 5000BP when elm, first, and then oak became less abundant. This change is laid at the door of Neolithic people who cleared land in order to pursue both pastoral and arable farming. As Fig. 3.1 shows, by 4000BP, Fife's woodland had been severely reduced, with grasses and sedges becoming more frequent along with a wide range of herbaceous species; ribwort plantain (*Plantago lanceolata*) became especially prominent at this time. This clearance of the woodland and the development of an intensively farmed landscape continued, with a hiatus during the Roman

period, right up to early modern times. It is only then that some landowners started to embellish their policies with trees and establish plantations, thus reversing the generally treeless nature of the Fife landscape.

A palaeosol from the Isle of Jura

Today, the vast majority of Jura is occupied by heather moorland, under which lie varying depths of blanket peat. Currently, exploitation of this area is for rough grazing for sheep and the cutting of peat to provide a domestic fuel supply. A very different situation obtained some 3-4000 years ago. The development of the peat has led to the fossilisation of a former cultural landscape. From time to time, the activity of crofters in peat cutting brings to light elements of this landscape. At Cul a'Bhaile, the appearance of massive stones extruding from cutover peat led to the discovery and subsequent excavation of a hut circle (Stevenson 1984). The peat development, which obscured this settlement feature, also caused the soil in existence at the time of the occupation of the hut to become fossilised and, as it is preserved under anaerobic conditions, the pollen record it contained is also preserved. The analysis of that record has produced pollen spectra (Fig. 3.2) which indicate a very different exploitative regime on Jura from that which is pursued today.

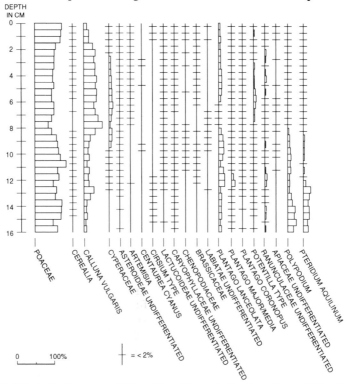

Fig 3.2: Selected pollen taxa, obtained from the analysis of a palaeosol taken from the enclosure which surrounded the hut circle at Cul a'Bhaile, Isle of Jura

As at present, there was very little woodland in existence, although hazel and alder did occur. What is striking is the strong presence of ribwort plantain, mugwort and other species, like fat hen (Chenopodiaceae), all of which can be associated with farming activities. That arable agriculture was once possible and undertaken in this area is clearly shown by the presence of cereal pollen. The lower part of the pollen diagram also indicates, in the presence of the spores of stag's horn moss (*Lycopodium clavatum*) and polypody (*Polypodium vulgare* [Plate 3.1a]), that manuring of the land took place, either with bedding or floor material from the house, or with litter from animal byres (Whittington 1988). There is evidence here not only of a very different agricultural regime but probably for a warmer climate than presently prevails in the Inner Hebrides.

Intertidal peats from the Uists, Outer Hebrides

The west coasts of the Isles of Uist are dominated by machair landscapes— beaches, dunes, slacks and plains (Ritchie 1979). They are backed by the so-called blacklands which are peat covered and only utilised for rough grazing of the heather and grass vegetation. The machair plains are more intensively used, being exploited for both arable and pastoral agriculture. Studies of the machair system show it has moved and still is moving inland, as coastal erosion re-mobilises the constituent sand and drives it eastwards. This present landscape, which is now considered to be a characteristic natural feature of the Outer Hebridean islands, is less than 5000 years old. Beyond the sand of the present beaches, it is possible to find, at low tide, in favoured, protected rocky areas, patches of peat (Fig. 3.3). These are only remnants of the sediment infills of once extensive freshwater lochs and dune slacks which have disappeared as the sea has encroached on the land since the last retreat of the ice. Pollen analysis of these peats shows that the character of these western landscapes of Scotland has undergone a fundamental change. Where, today, there are shallow seas, extensive beaches, and the dunes and plains which make up the machair system, there were, until 5000BP, extensive woodlands, as shown by the pollen spectra from An Ceòthan on Benbecula (Fig. 3.4). They consisted mainly of birch, hazel and willow, although it is possible that oak and elm, as minor constituents, were also present.

Plant irruptions in environmental change

Within the last decade or so, many landscapes have undergone a sudden and, to some, unwelcome and undesirable change. The introduction of a new agricultural crop, oilseed rape, has been criticised as besmirching the delicate colours of our countryside, ruining honey production and causing unprecedented outbreaks of hayfever. Have there been new plant irruptions before and what effect did they have upon our environment? Analysis of lacustrine muds, from Black Loch in north Fife and from Kilconquhar Loch in east Fife, show that, from the tenth or eleventh century AD, the occupants of Fife had to come to terms with the sudden arrival of a new plant in their landscape. Who was responsible for the introduction of hemp (*Cannabis sativa*) is not known, but from the pollen record (Fig. 3.5) it is clear that it became a

Fig 3.3: The location of inter-tidal peats in the Uists and adjacent islands

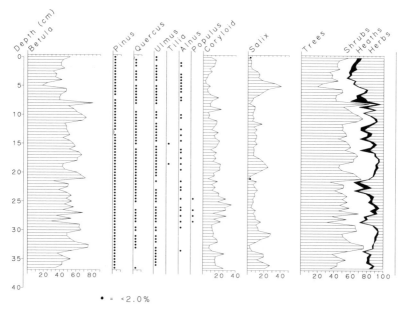

Fig 3.4: Arboreal pollen taxa values and total pollen summary from an inter-tidal peat
at An Ceòthan, Benbecula, Outer Hebrides

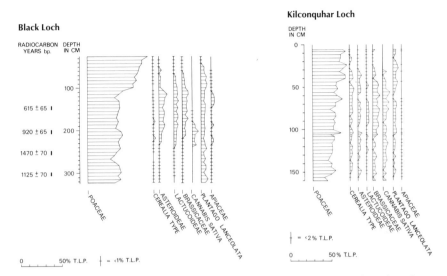

Fig 3.5: Selected pollen taxa, related to farming activities around Black Loch and Kilconquhar Loch, Fife

significant crop in the arable husbandry of Fife. What is also interesting is the difference in time over which it was cultivated at the two sites. Around Black Loch, it was prominent for about three centuries and then it vanished, as abruptly as it had appeared. At Kilconquhar Loch, it remained in cultivation for a much longer period, perhaps stimulated by the demand for its fibre in the manufacture of sails and ropes for the extensive fishing fleet of the East Neuk. The history of this, until recently, unrecognised cultivar in medieval Scotland is still far from clear (Edwards and Whittington 1990) and would have remained virtually entirely unknown without the evidence obtained from pollen analysis. Its introduction must, however, have had a major impact upon the farming and craft environments; whether it also had an effect upon the social environment as well will probably never be known.

Conclusion

These are just a few out of the many examples of change to Scotland's environment that have occurred and which pollen analysis has made accessible. It can be shown that the decline in elm trees, brought about in recent times by Dutch elm disease, is not an isolated or new phenomenon in Scotland (Whittington et al 1991b). Even more surprising changes can be demonstrated; who, for example, would have thought that holly (*Ilex aquifolium*) was once a major constituent of the flora of upland Nairnshire (Walker et al 1992) or that *Bruckenthalia spiculifolia*, an ericaceous plant which now grows only in the uplands of Greece, Turkey, Romania,

Yugoslavia and Bulgaria, had in the past grown in Shetland (Birks and Peglar 1979) and Aberdeenshire (Whittington, *unpubl.*)? Pollen analysis, despite the many problems which its practitioners readily recognise, provides an extremely powerful tool for unlocking the enormous environmental changes that Scotland has witnessed, some of which are, at present, almost certainly still unknown to us.

Bibliography

Barber K E. 1981. *Peat Stratigraphy and Climatic Change*. Balkema, Rotterdam

Birks H J B, Peglar S M. 1979. Interglacial pollen spectra from Sel Ayre, Shetland. *New Phytologist* 83: 559-75

Bottema S. 1975. The interpretation of pollen spectra from prehistoric settlements (with special attention to Liguliflorae). *Palaeohistoria* 17: 17-35

Brazier V, Whittington G, Ballantyne C K. 1988. Holocene debris cone evolution in Glen Etive, Western Grampian Highlands, Scotland. *Earth Surface Processes and Landforms* 13: 525-31

Clymo R S. 1991. Peat growth. In: Shane L C K, Cushing E J (eds). *Quaternary Landscapes*. Belhaven Press, London

Cundill P R, Whittington G. 1983. Anomalous arboreal pollen assemblages in Late Devensian and Early Flandrian deposits at Creich Castle, Fife, Scotland. *Boreas* 12: 297-313

Davis M B, Brubaker L B. 1969. Differential sedimentation of pollen grains in lakes. *Limnology and Oceanography* 18: 635-46

Davis M B, Moeller R E, Ford J. 1984. Sediment focusing and pollen influx. In: Haworth E Y, Lund J W G (eds). *Lake Sediments and Environmental History*. Leicester University Press, Leicester

Edwards K J, Whittington G. 1990. Palynological evidence for the growing of *Cannabis sativa* L. (hemp) in medieval and historical Scotland. *Transactions of the Institute of British Geographers*. NS 15: 60-69

Edwards K J, Whittington G. 1993. Aspects of the environmental and depositional history of a rock basin in eastern Scotland. In: McManus J, Duck R W (eds). *Geomorphology and Sedimentology of Lakes and Reservoirs*. John Wiley, Chichester

Havinga A J. 1984. A 20-year experimental investigation into the differential corrosion susceptibility of pollen and spores in various soil types. *Pollen et Spores* 26: 541-58

Moore P D, Webb J A, Collinson M E. 1991. *Pollen Analysis*. 2nd edn. Blackwell Scientific Publications, Oxford

Ritchie W. 1979. Machair development and chronology in the Uists and adjacent islands. *Proceedings of the Royal Society of Edinburgh*. 77B: 107-22

Stevenson J B. 1984. The excavation of a hut circle at Cul a'Bhaile, Jura. *Proceedings of the Society of Antiquaries of Scotland* 114: 147-57

Tyldesley J B. 1973. Long-range transmission of tree pollen to Shetland. *New Phytologist* 72: 175-81; 183-90; 691-97

Walker M J C, Merritt J W et al. 1992. Allt Odhar and Dalcharn: two pre-Late Devensian/Weichselian sites in northern Scotland. *Journal of Quaternary Science* 7: 69-86

Whittington G. 1988. Environmental reconstruction at Cul a'Bhaile, Isle of Jura. In: Bintliff J L, Davidson D A, Grant E G (eds). *Conceptual Issues in Environmental Archaeology*. Edinburgh University Press, Edinburgh

Whittington G, Gordon A D. 1987. The differentiation of the pollen of *Cannabis sativa* L. from that of *Humulus lupulus* L. *Pollen et Spores* 29: 111-20

Whittington G, Edwards K J, Cundill P R. 1991a. Late- and post-glacial vegetational change at Black Loch, Fife, eastern Scotland—a multiple core approach. *New Phytologist* 118: 147-66

Whittington G, Edwards K J, Cundill P R. 1991b. Palaeoecological investigations of multiple elm declines at a site in north Fife, Scotland. *Journal of Biogeography* 18: 71-87

Further reading:

For a more extensive introduction to pollen analysis:

Birks H J B, Birks H H. 1980. *Quaternary Palaeoecology*. Edward Arnold, London.

Dimbleby G W. 1985. *The Playnology of Archaeological Sites*. Academic Press, London

For reports on the use of pollen analysis on particular sites see, for example:

Journal of Archaeological Science; Journal of Biogeography; Journal of Ecology; New Phytologist; The Holocene. These in turn will lead back to many other related papers.

4

WOODLAND HISTORY BEFORE 1850

Chris Smout

Introduction

There was a time after the final retreat of the last ice sheet from Scotland when invading trees covered all the land that was neither bog, mountain top nor fresh water loch, with primeval forest. They did not arrive immediately on the bare tundra. Aspen and birch would come first, pine and oak later. The evidence is that Scots pine in the Highlands appeared about 8000 years ago in the far north west and took millennia to work their way south to Glen Falloch and north to Caithness, though there was also early Scots pine in parts of the Lowlands such as Fife and Galloway. The highest known treelines in Cairngorm, at about 2,600 feet, were reached in a period of climatic optimum about 5000BC (Dickson 1992). Mesolithic people arrived at roughly the same time as the pine, both alien species. At the time of maximum woodland cover—perhaps 6000 to 4000 years ago—we might imagine that 50 to 60 percent of the land surface was covered with natural woodland. At present—and this is about the only other relatively uncontested fact—natural woodland covers only one or two per cent of the whole.

Until recently it was assumed that, when the Romans arrived, the primeval forest would still have been close to its original widest bounds, with only minor inroads made upon it by early man: and that they fought their way through densely wooded Lowlands, before being ultimately brought to a halt by a Great Wood of Caledon somewhere beyond the Antonine Wall (Anderson 1967; Darling 1947). In this mythology, it was the Romans who really began the great destruction by felling, burning and clearing: the Vikings continued the work, burning forests to clear out their enemies; medieval barons, like the Wolf of Badenoch and Robert the Bruce, were credited with the same. By the end of the Middle Ages, the forest cover had gone in the Lowlands, which became renowned for their treelessness, but the Great Wood of Caledon in the north was supposed to have been only affected to a minor degree. Its ultimate destruction was supposed to be the work of Cromwell's soldiers—again with axe and fire—and then of English ironmasters and building speculators, finally with the *coup de grace* administered by Lowland sheepmasters in the nineteenth century. Almost all the villains were foreigners or outsiders. Fraser Darling linked this interpretation to a point about the development of an external market:

> Man does not seem to extirpate a feature of his environment as long as that natural resource is concerned only with man's everyday life: but as soon as he looks upon it as having some value for export—that he can live by selling it to some distant populations—there is real danger.

Research within the last two decades has in several respects very much modified this approach, without by any means clearing up all of the problems involved.

Firstly, pollen analysis has established that widespread, though not necessarily universal, disafforestation had occurred in the Lowlands long before the Romans arrived; other archaeological methods reach the same conclusions (see Chapters 3 & 6, this volume; Tipping 1993). In the Highlands, too, Scots pine had retreated from Caithness before 1000BC, and cultivation was already widespread in many parts—for example in Speyside (Gear and Huntley 1992; O'Sullivan 1977).

Secondly, the Great Wood of Caledon itself has recently been seen less as a concrete description of a Scottish forest than as a metaphor and excuse for military failure (Breeze 1992). Once the original texts are analysed, a better case can probably be made out for a great bog of Caledon than a great wood of Caledon, for the Romans were more obviously impressed by the ability of the natives to merge into the marshland than into any woodland cover. Simple observations suggest something wrong with the traditional account. For example, the line of Roman signal stations along the old road by Findo Gask, west of Perth, should command a view of Strathearn to the south and Glenalmond to the North, but not a thing can be seen from them today because they are swathed about with modern conifer plantations. In Roman times they must have surveyed open country from a bare ridge.

Thirdly, the sheer improbability of the traditional account is evident. How on earth could the Romans, the Vikings or a feudal baronage destroy a wood with axe and fire? Even if soldiers had ever felled large areas of trees, armies move on and woodland regenerates: if they torched a pine wood, it would have provided a perfect seed-bed for a new one, and if they had tried to set alight living oak and birch they would never have succeeded without naphtalm.

That natural woodland in the Lowlands had been reduced to very small proportions by 1600 appears incontrovertible, and the need for substantial imports of Norwegian and later Swedish and Baltic timber to fill the gap left by disafforestation reinforces other evidence. Woodland cover, it has recently been maintained, had been reduced from its maximum of, say, 50 percent of the entire Scottish land surface in Mesolithic times to 5 percent or less in the seventeenth century (Walker and Kirby 1989). There are, of course, two ways of considering that broadbrush judgement, if it is true: one is to say that nine-tenths of the natural woodland had already gone before the Union of Crowns: the other is to say that even 5 percent is four or five times as much natural wood as exists at the present day. If nine-tenths had vanished by

1600, it cannot be true that the main culprits were outsiders, unless we attribute almost supernatural powers to the Romans and the Vikings. Lastly in this particular context, even if we accept that there had been a decline of forest cover from 50 percent to 5 percent of the whole, we have no idea of when most of this happened in a time span of about 5000 years, or if it was a linear process rather than, as seems much more likely, one in which the forest cover would retreat in some epochs and advance at others.

Major factors affecting forest cover

Climate

The period 5500-3000BC was one of climatic optimum for tree growth throughout Europe, but in Scotland and Ireland the rapid spread of peat over much previously afforested land in the following millennia was associated with deteriorating weather: this has been clearly traced from, for example, Loch Maree at about 2200BC (Birks 1972). The extent to which human intervention tipped the scales towards the formation of blanket peat due to the destruction of forest cover, and how far this was an inevitable natural process, is still unclear (Simmons and Tooley 1981). The period of the late Iron Age and Roman invasion apparently saw a warmer and drier climate again, but from about 400AD several centuries of intense cold in Northern Europe supervened. The twelfth and thirteenth centuries were warm and dry, with vineyards established in the south of England and cultivation possible at 1000 feet altitude and higher in the Southern Uplands of Scotland. They were followed from the fourteenth to the seventeenth centuries by the so-called 'Little Ice Age' of climatology, with strong winds, heavy rains, unseasonable cold and frequent crop failures (Morrison 1993; Lamb 1977). Periods of increasing rainfall and stronger winds are likely to be inimical in Scotland to tree cover, though more rain might favour some species (like alder) at the expense of others (like Scots pine). The importance of this climatic variation can be seen in any forest, even in the recent past, as witness the evidence that ancient pines in the west find greater difficulty in setting seed than those of similar age in the east, due to the extent of peat formation beneath them. The forest archaeology of the Black Wood of Rannoch has traced periods in which moisture-loving species like alder have flourished more than at other times (Steven and Carlisle 1959; Hayer 1967).

Rural population

Periods of demographic pressure on the countryside, (such as the thirteenth century, 1550-1650 or 1750-1850), have an inevitable impact on woodland, whether it is through the tooth and hoof of cattle, sheep and goats (an extremely widespread domestic animal in the traditional Highlands), or through the axe and plough of farmers converting forest into arable. More people lead to less forest: and a decline in population to recovery in forest cover. However, with increasing population there could also come a point at which the value of the forest (for fuel, building timber or stock shelter), could come to be more highly appreciated if other sources of these materials were lacking, and the erosion of forest might stop. If there were convenient alternatives (peat for firewood, stone and turf for building timber, stone walls for shelter) this safeguard, however, might fail.

External demand for wood, bark and charcoal

Fraser Darling's assumption was that this demand would lead to unsustainable exploitation. Under some circumstances it might: the use of the Loch Ewe and Loch Maree woodlands by the seventeenth-century ironmaster Sir George Hay may fall in this category, though the felling of a deciduous wood would instantly be followed by regeneration unless there was another cause preventing it—such as conversion to arable or heavy grazing pressure by peasant animals or sheepmasters' flocks. On the other hand, historians until comparatively recently overlooked traditions of sustainable management through fencing and coppicing, such as were extensively practised in oak woods along Loch Awe and Loch Lomond where the woods were used in the eighteenth and nineteenth centuries by the ironmasters and tanbarkers (Tittensor 1970; Rymer 1980; Lindsay 1975a,b), or of fencing and limited cutting as practised in the native pinewoods at Rannoch and Speyside. Here we have a coincidence of heavy exploitation and extensive survival. The fact that these woods had a value placed upon them by the market was the cause not of their destruction but of their preservation. As observed by a contemporary at the peak of their intensive exploitation, Dunbartonshire oak woods, harvested on a 20-year rotation, yielded 'a much higher rent than could be got for the ground if put to any other purpose, for in general it is unfit for tillage or, if laid under pasture, it would not give much' (Ure 1794). Woodland like this became neglected and degraded again when chemical substitutes for natural tannin, and mineral coal substitutes for charcoal, removed that premium. Then the animals were let in, and the wood deteriorated.

The widest extent of surviving semi-natural woodland is on land that, firstly, has no great value for arable agriculture and secondly, is reasonably accessible. Thus the oak woods of Argyll, Dunbartonshire and Perthshire are extensive, as is the native pine of the Cairngorms area: much smaller and in worse condition are those fragments protected solely by their remoteness, like the Scots pines of Loch Tulla or the native birch of Strathnavar.

The value of land under wood, of course, must always be seen in the context of alternative land use. It was always a matter of opportunity cost. The effect of the rising profitability of wool exports from the monastic and other estates of southern Scotland was seen in the Middle Ages in the manifest decline in woodland in the royal and baronial hunting 'forests' of parts of the Southern Uplands (Anderson 1967), and has also recently been traced on monastic lands in the area between the Urr and the Nith, where grants of pannage before around 1180 (implying herds of pigs and cattle in an oak forest) gave way abruptly to grants of pasture for sheep (Oram 1989; and *pers comm*). Between 1327 and 1332, 5,700 sacks of Scottish wool were exported annually (360lbs of wool per sack). The trade peaked at 7,360 sacks in 1370-74. With each medieval Scottish sheep providing one to two pounds of wool, it seems probable that in the late thirteenth century some 1,500,000-2,500,000 sheep may have been grazed to supply the Scottish wool clip exported to Flanders (Grant 1984). This statistic needs to be kept in proportion. The animals would have been very small compared to their modern equivalents: most of the Lowlands were still farmed by peasants uninvolved in this commerce: and at this stage in Scottish history, commercial sheep farming did not impinge on the Highlands at all.

Quality of woodland management

The kind of 'woodmanship' identified by Rackham (1980) in the ancient semi-natural woodlands of England (and France) can be dimly detected in the Scottish Lowlands among the oaks at Cadzow, Mugdock and Dalkeith: occasional grants, such as to Lindores Abbey in 1250 for a hundred loads of hazel rods annually, imply systematic coppicing, and Gilbert presented evidence for medieval Baron Courts carefully controlling woodcutting on their lands (Dickson 1992; Stevenson 1990; Rackham 1986). When Richard de Lincoln in 1250 allowed the monks of Kelso to take timber for building repairs from his wood in Mow on condition that they gave that wood 20-30 years to recover, he was trying to manage the timber in a 'sustainable' way (Gilbert 1979). Similarly, when the Earl of Cawdor in the seventeenth century sold his oaks on condition that their purchasers left the young trees unharmed, he was exercising good stewardship of his woods. The present Great Wood of Cawdor is presumably the result. On the other hand his neighbours, the Earls of Moray—a family of much greater political ambition —appear to have cut out the original forest of Darnaway in some moment of great financial need, and only tiny fragments remain in a gorge (W Mutch *pers comm*). Then, as now, the quality of land management varied over time.

In the Highlands, good forest management was practised on Clanranald lands long before the eighteenth century (see Ch. 5 this volume); that it was not isolated can be seen from seventeenth-century regulations on tree planting and muirburn in the Baron Court of Glenorchy (Innes 1855). It is entirely likely that in the remnant Caledonian pine forests there would have been some wood-pasture regime—the open crowns of Scottish granny pines themselves suggest they had grown in semi-cleared ground. When we get to the eighteenth century, professional estate foresters like William Lorimer on Speyside, ensured good quality management where wood was regarded as valuable. The points of danger lay when either no-one judged it worth the cost to preserve the wood (if it was more valuable as cleared pasture), or where communal controls were too weak to prevent a classic 'tragedy of the commons'—the peasants knew the wood was a valuable resource, but also knew that if they as individuals did not quickly exercise a right to cut, someone would get there first, and no community control was strong enough to stop unsustainable exploitation. This appeared to be the situation developing in Strathspey in the 1760s to which Lorimer responded by control from the landlord's side (Dickson 1975, 1976).

Forest cover since the Romans

Is it possible, with the help of the four factors listed above, to discover or guess the likely course of forest-cover history since the departure of the Romans? The answer must as yet be 'only very dimly'. In Fife there are signs of forests returning in the course of the Roman era, perhaps a consequence of declining population brought about by war or disease. We have so little evidence of the course of population history in the next millennium as to be very uneasy about even guessing how far the forests may have come back, or how far they may have retreated again. It is possible, again in Fife, to find evidence of renewed forest retreat associated with cultivation in what may broadly be described as Pictish times, around 500AD (Whittington et al 1990). Not everywhere was the same. The latest surveys of the Forest of Mar—surely always one of the wildest areas in the whole of Scotland—shows no surviving sign of prehistoric settlement, but clear evidence of settlement at some late medieval or early modern date. Only excavation could enable it to be dated more exactly. On the other hand, the uplands of north-east Perthshire are a palimpsest of prehistoric settlement, probably cleared of trees and farmed or managed since the Early Bronze Age, and also include what may well prove to be Pictish farms. Their survival, undisturbed by the roots of regenerating trees, shows this land to have been open country for thousands of years (Ch. 6 this volume).

A rich continuing fauna, some of it associated with woodland, is indicated by the animals carved on Pictish stones: wolves, wild boar, deer, eagles and salmon, with—as in the hunting scene on the Drostan stone—occasional brown bear and a creature that might represent wild cattle. We know the Romans sent a Caledonian bear to the circus in Rome; the species probably did not survive in Scotland into medieval times. On the other hand, we know that the European beaver did, from its appearance in the reign of David I in a book of tolls levied on exported skins, a list which also included the more familiar fox, otter, wild cat and pine marten. The same list of animals is still mentioned by Hector Boece in 1527 as around Loch Ness, and sought by foreign merchants at Inverness (Brown 1893). The survival of the beaver is especially interesting from our perspective, as to survive it needs open deciduous woods, such as oak, ash, alder, willow, poplar and birch (with undergrowth) situated alongside lochs or rivers. It was not an animal of the Caledonian pine.

Place name evidence is another potentially useful guide to the extent of former afforestation, but this is usually hard to date with accuracy. Both Drumlanrig and Lanark imply clearances in woodland, presumably of a very early date, and Kincardine is a Pictish place-name indicating the 'end of the thicket wood'. Keith was an ancient word for woodland, and woods survived at Keith in Aberdeenshire until the end of the Middle Ages; the Earl Marischal expelled a tenant from his holding in 1488 for unlawfully grubbing up part of them for arable use (Gilbert 1979). Place-name evidence in the Grampians (Edlin 1959) reveals former woods at an elevation well above the present tree line; since they are Gaelic and not Pictish these names were presumably acquired in the ninth century or later.

A high tree line probably reflects an age of better climate than our own, and therefore a period of greater potential for upland cultivation, such as the thirteenth century when oats could be cultivated on the tops of the Lammermuirs. That same century was also a period of population pressure, land reclamation and pressure on the woods, as evidenced in the Lowlands and Southern Uplands from proliferation of settlements and the spread of monastic sheep farming. The Black Death in 1349, and subsequent outbreaks of plague, should have taken pressure off the woods, but Gilbert (1979) notes that north of the Tay there is little sign of this, perhaps because disease affected scattered rural populations less severely. In any case the Little Ice Age, commencing at around the same time, might both have created a poor natural environment for woodland regeneration (especially in the west), and forced the population to rely for their own subsistence on more extensive (as opposed to intensive) husbandry on outfields, and on larger animal herds. It is interesting in this context that whereas John of Fordun, writing around 1380, could still speak from hearsay of 'vast woods, full of stags, roe-deer, and other wild animals and beasts of various kinds' along the foot of the Highland mountains, and say that they were large enough for the inhabitants to hide their cattle in from the depredations of strangers, when Hector Boece came early in the sixteenth century to speak of a Great Wood of Caledon he located it in the remotest antiquity; he regarded the contemporary Highlands as wild and full of wolves but (like other commentators and travellers) he had little to say about forests (Skene 1872; Brown 1893). The wolf would have been a characteristic pest of extensive animal husbandry associated with a scattered human population. Scottish medieval historians have not found evidence for trees regenerating on deserted farming ground such as has been found in late medieval Norway and France.

Signs of timber scarcities in some areas can be found as early as the thirteenth century (Gilbert 1979), but 'only in the fifteenth century is there evidence for serious shortage of timber in large areas of Scotland'. By 1600 the Lowlands were largely denuded, and evidence for the Highlands in the sketch maps of Timothy Pont (Stone 1989; Smout 1991) similarly suggests that the original cover had also by then very largely disappeared. With human population rising rapidly again after about 1550, the beaver and the wild boar, already rare in the late Middle Ages, disappeared, and the wolf had also become exterminated before the end of the seventeenth century.

In the seventeenth, eighteenth and early nineteenth centuries, the decline of the surviving woods, particularly of oak, began, however, to be checked by improved management and higher values. Such management was species selective—in oakwoods, the oak was preferred to species like ash, rowan or holly, so 'naturalness' and diversity must have suffered. But the woodland regimes, at their best, were perfectly sustainable. In addition substantial increases were made to the acreage under wood by artificial plantations of Scots pine, beech and larch, in particular, by improving landowners wishing to decorate their policies.

On the other hand human population in the countryside, especially of the Highlands and in spite of the clearances, was never higher than in the century 1750-1850, and the pressure on ill-managed woods, or those regarded as being of little value, would have been more intense than ever before. In a fascinating 'Plan for a Royal forest of oak in the Highlands of Scotland' (a scheme of the 1780s which foreshadows the campaigns of Reforesting Scotland), John Williams (1784) describes some of that pressure. There are, he says, on the lands of the Duke of Gordon in Lochaber, and on the annexed former Jacobite estates in Ross, Inverness and Argyll, 'a great many thousand acres' which

> form a rich stool of oak in a deep soil, where the most luxuriant shoots are produced in summer, while the goats are in the hills; but they are soon browsed down in autumn, and kept level with the heath, by the goats and other cattle; and if any plant chances to raise its head beyond the reach of the goats, it is soon destroyed by the axe of the Highlandman, who strips off about four feet of the bark quite round, a little above the root, and leaves the young tree standing, to die a lingering death, as a monument of his barbarous greed.

He lists among such lands, Coigach, the north side of Lochbroom, Kinlochmoidart, 'several thousand acres' of the north shore of Loch Eil, and 'in the glens at the head' of Loch Eil, in Glen Lochy and along Loch Lochy, around Loch Arkaig 'beautifully and richly covered with oak, birch and fir, where a good deal of oak is grown out of the reach of cattle'. He adds to this the north shore of Loch Leven, with 'a good stoop of oak', Ardshiel—'and a good deal peeps out of the heath on the braes of that estate, in summer'—as well as parts of Speyside, and 'a thick stool of oak appears among the heath, over great part of that extensive moor, which is situated between Fort William and the river Spey'. He seems to be describing the death agony of a natural forest misused by tenants and neglected by landlords as a thing of no value.

In contrast to this, he praises the woods of Ardnamurchan, south-west Perth and north-west Argyll, 'well enclosed and improved', and used for charcoal or tanbark in a commercial and sustainable manner; he blames the neglect of the north-west on 'great graziers' who have innumerable herds, subtenants and cottars, 'and every one of these dependants has a flock of goats, and every man an ax, both for cutting fewel, and for peeling bark to tan his leather'. We are not yet, be it noted, in the age of sheep farms in this area; the 'great graziers' run cattle.

In this situation of heavy pressure, woodland fauna obviously suffered. The Scottish capercaillie was lost in these years, victim of being a large and obvious game bird in a dwindling natural environment full of hungry people. The goshawk, another forest bird, apparently went at the same time; the great spotted woodpecker also disappeared; the red squirrel was reduced to very low numbers. The numbers of red deer were also much below what they had been in earlier times and what they later became (see Chapter 8 this volume).

Charles St John, writing of Morayshire in 1847, has an interesting observation on woodcock—'a few years ago, it was supposed that none remained in Britain after the end of the winter, except a few wounded birds. However, since the great increase of fir plantations, great numbers remain to breed'. This suggests that the new conifer planting was beginning to redeem some of the decline in natural woodland. He went on to describe the new woods of Altyre and Darnaway, 'as well as in all the other extensive plantations in the country', as containing 'considerable numbers' of woodcock in the nesting season (St John 1847). When the capercaillie and the red squirrel were reintroduced, and the great spotted woodpecker reinvaded, there was enough planted Scots pine to supplement the remnants of original woodland and maintain their populations.

Disaster for many of the remaining managed semi-natural woods became inevitable in the nineteenth century, when wood products were cheaply imported or metal and chemical substitutes were found for them. At the same time the value of ground under pasture did not decline, or at least did not decline to the same degree. Sheep farming became more general and more intense, until it was partly replaced by the maintenance of estates for deer. These herbivores prevented regeneration in felled or grubbed-up woods; they also grazed off the seedlings under most of the surviving semi-natural woods, but without reducing their potential as a source of seed.

Conclusion

Modern ecologists, when they inspect surviving ancient Scottish woodland, universally deplore its widespread failure to regenerate. The problem is reversible by removing grazing pressure, providing seed-bearing trees survive. Woods can make a comeback after even two centuries of neglect. What we observe now is not new but must have been seen many times in the past, as the woods over the ages ceased to regenerate through the activities of the grazing animals. Most probably eventually collapsed of their own accord, rather than being felled in an act of dramatic clearance. Thus the decay of woods was long drawn-out, slow, inexorable; and the main agents responsible, perhaps, at first the altering climate, then the indigenous farmer's need for land, only comparatively seldom the external capitalist's need for profit—and never the mad invader's fire and sword.

Bibliography

Acts of the Parliament of Scotland. Vol 1. Appendix 3.
Anderson M. 1967. *A History of Scottish Forestry.* Nelson, Edinburgh
Birks H H. 1972. Studies in the vegetational history of Scotland III: A radio-carbon pollen diagram from Loch Maree, Ross and Cromarty. *New Phytologist* 71: 731-54
Breeze D J. 1992. The great myth of Caledon. *Scottish Forestry* 46: 331-35
Brown P Hume. 1893. *Scotland Before 1700 from Contemporary Documents.* Edinburgh
Darling F Fraser. 1947. *Natural History in the Highlands and Islands.* Collins, London
Dickson G A. 1975. William Lorimer on forestry in the Central Highlands in the early 1760s. *Scottish Forestry* 29: 191-210
Dickson G A. 1976. Forestry in Speyside in the 1760s. *Scottish Forestry* 30: 38-60

Dickson J H. 1992. Scottish woodlands: their ancient past and precarious future. *Botanical Journal of Scotland*: 26

Gear A J, Huntley B. 1992. Rapid changes in the range limits of Scots pine 4000 years ago. *Science* 251: 544-47

Gilbert J. 1979. *Hunting and Hunting Reserves in Medieval Scotland*. John Donald, Edinburgh

Grant A. 1984. *Independence and Nationhood*. London

Hayer A J. 1967. Palaeoecology of Black Wood of Rannoch. *Scottish Forestry* 21: 157-62

Innes C (ed.) 1855. *The Black Book of Taymouth*. Bannatyne Club, Edinburgh

Lamb H H. 1977. *Climates: Present, Past and Future*. Methuen, London

Lindsay J M. 1975a. Charcoal iron smelting and its fuel supply: the example of Lorn furnace, Argyllshire, 1753-1876. *Journal of Historical Geography* I.

Lindsay J M. 1975b. Timber supply in the Scottish Highlands. *Scottish Studies* 19: 39-53

Morrison I. 1993. Unpublished lecture, Scottish Medievalist's conference, Pitlochry.

Oram R. 1989. The Lordship of Galloway, c1000 to c1250. Unpublished PhD thesis, University of St Andrews

O'Sullivan P E. 1977. Vegetation history and the native pine woods. In: Bunce R G H, Jeffary J N R. 1977. *Native Pinewoods of Scotland*. ITE, Cambridge

Rackham O. 1980. *Ancient Woodland: its History, Vegetation and Uses in England*. Edward Arnold, London

Rackham O. 1986. *The History of the Countryside*. Dent, London

Rymer L. 1980. Recent woodland history of North Knapdale. *Scottish Forestry* 34: 244-56

St John C 1847. *Short Sketches of the Wild Sports and Natural History of the Highlands*. London

Simmons I G, Tooley M J (eds). 1981. *The Environment in British Prehistory*. Duckworth, London

Skene W F (ed). 1872. *John of Fordun's Chronicle of the Scottish Nation*. Vol. 1. Edinburgh

Smout T C. 1991. Highland land use before 1800: misconceptions, evidence and realities. In: Bachell A (ed). 1991. *Highland Land Use: Four Historical and Conservation Perspectives*. NCCS, Inverness

Steven H M, Carlisle A. 1959. *The Native Pinewoods of Scotland*. Oliver & Boyd, Edinburgh

Stevenson J. 1990. How ancient is the woodland of Mugdock? *Scottish Forestry* 44: 161-72

Stone J C. 1989. *The Pont Manuscript maps of Scotland: Sixteenth-century Origins of a Blaeu Atlas*. Map Productions, Tring

Tipping R 1993. A "History of the Scottish Forests" revisited. *Reforesting Scotland* 8: 16-21; 9: 18-21

Tittensor R M. 1970. History of the Loch Lomond oakwoods. *Scottish Forestry* 24: 100-18

Ure T 1894. *General View of the Agriculture of the County of Dumbarton*.

Walker G J, Kirby K J. 1989. *Inventories of Ancient, Long-established and Semi-natural Woodland for Scotland*. NCC, Research & Survey in Nature Conservation Series No. 22

Whittington G, Edwards, K J, Cundill P R. 1990. *Palaeoenvironmental investigations at Black Loch in the Ochil hills of Fife, Scotland*. O'Dell Memorial Monograph, 22, University of Aberdeen

Williams J. 1784. Plans for a Royal forest of oak in the highlands of Scotland. *Archaeologica Scotica*. Vol. 1: 29

5

WOODLANDS ON THE CLANRANALD ESTATES
A Case Study

Hugh Cheape

The comment has been made that the landscape is a document and the hardest of all documents to read, succeeding generations writing something on its defenceless surface until it becomes an almost indecipherable palimpsest. This would be truer perhaps of the English countryside than of the relatively inhospitable west coast of Scotland on which, we imagine, the impressions left by man on a mountainous landscape sculpted by intense glacial activity are less obtrusive.

If the hand of man is less obvious in the West Highlands, history may not seem so important or useful for the interpretation of the natural environment. But the proposition is usually made that the landscape has suffered long term, progressive degradation from a verdant paradise to produce the appearance of wilderness familiar to us today in much of the West Highlands. Environmental issues therefore have an historical dimension which is perhaps the subject of misapprehension or misinterpretation.

To know and understand the past is not simple and history on the ground is often the least intelligible. Explanations of the historical process will necessarily depend on generalisations which never reveal the whole truth (insofar as such is approachable) and may even lead us into error. To understand the natural environment it is necessary to enlist history, and it may be helpful to proceed from the particular to the general in order to read the landscape document to best effect. Woodlands on the Clanranald Estates in the West Highlands provide an example of history on the ground and its complexities.

The conventional wisdom winning general acceptance is that much of Britain, to the extent of about two-thirds, was in prehistory covered by forests of oak and ash, together with beech, alder and hazel. About 5,000 years ago, woodland began to be cleared for cultivation and pasture, and by *ca.*1000AD in England and the twelfth century in Scotland, most British forests, at least in the Lowlands, had gone (Anderson 1967; Steven and Carlisle 1959; Darling 1947, 1955). Primeval wood that survived clearance and colonisation is now of the greatest importance for the conservation of

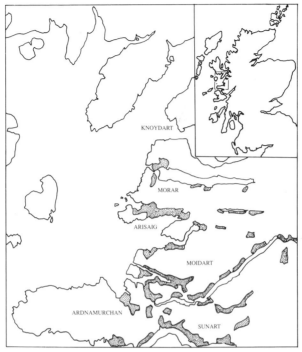

Fig 5.1: Woodlands on Clanranald's mainland estates

wildlife and natural habitat in Britain and is rightly attracting the keenest attention and measures for its protection. The natural vegetation of the west coast area of Scotland was originally broadleaved woodland and some areas of relatively extensive oak woods of this quality still survive in the West Highlands. We presume that they are remnants of a natural forest cover which once covered large parts of the Highlands from the West Coast through the Great Glen to the Moray Firth. We also presume that the erosion of this natural forest has been persistent and carried on into the twentieth century without regard to ecological considerations. A description of the fate of indigenous oak woods on an island in the River Beauly in Strathglass at the end of the eighteenth century would be accepted as typical of the long term pattern of man's profligacy:

> The island is generally wooded with birch and oak, and at one period it was covered with very fine oaks, some of which were of large girth, measuring about twenty feet in circumference. These were all exchanged with the Laird of Struy for some houses in Inverness, and cut down about forty years since. (Carruthers 1843)

We should sound a note of caution in interpreting the past of the environment. An assumed erosion of the natural forest cover may not have been so persistent, even, or widespread. Historically oak-birch woodland was despoiled and locally exploited for fuel, for tanning, or for other raw materials, but there is scattered evidence to suggest that from the medieval to the early modern period it was a managed resource on the Clanranald Estates and valued separately from the other elements of land ownership and its use and exploitation strictly controlled.

The area (Fig 5.1) deserves close study for its almost unique characteristics. The Clanranald Estates are of great significance geographically, spanning more than a hundred miles from Atlantic *machair* in the Uists to the 'Rough Bounds' of mainland Inverness-shire, politically as a surviving element of the former Lordship of the Isles, and culturally as a conservative society relatively isolated from processes of acculturation from the east and south, yet maintaining links through the Roman Catholic Church, education and military service with the Continent. Conventionally we would approach an historical analysis by an evaluation of the documentary record, the locus of which is to the south and east, either in Edinburgh or in Westminster. In studying Hebridean history we should try to shift the centre of gravity from east to west to sense an almost baroque grandeur of a society in its own sub-oceanic culture-province but moving outward with ease to other parts of Europe.

Clanranald woods in Moidart and Arisaig are now fragmented, reflecting, on the one hand, different patterns of occupancy and grazing in the long term and, on the other hand, serious failure of natural regeneration in the last 150 years. Many of the larger trees must be now about 80 years old and over. The mature trees are in the age bracket of 120-150 years and a few are undoubtedly over 200 years old. Tree cover extends from sea level to about 300 metres with the densest woodland on the steeper sloping ground. Oak is the main species in these woods, and birch and alder are well represented with occasional ash and elm and a sparse understorey of holly, hazel, willow and rowan. The potential for regeneration is very good and perhaps better than other west coast oakwoods. The trees are prolific by nature, as demonstrated by stands of young oak and birch in enclosures at Glenfinnan on the eastern edge of the area. Around Glenfinnan itself, there are old stands of native Scots pine (Pl.5.1) which were referred to in early eighteenth-century Gaelic song in terms of their economic as well as aesthetic value (MacDonald and MacDonald 1924 pp. 262, 400). References in literary contexts may reflect traditions of oak, yew and rowan being sacred woods.

Most of the Clanranald woodlands are now designated as Sites of Special Scientific Interest (SSSI) under the review procedure of 'renotification'. This is timely recognition of their particular and almost unique character and reflects a welcome shift in official interest since, formerly, few of these woodlands were included in the *Nature Conservation Review* of 1977. The woods shelter a rich and exceptional range of oceanic flora and vegetation, such as very rare species of mosses and liverworts; there is a rich assemblage of Atlantic species of liverwort of very limited distribution, with examples almost unknown elsewhere.

The woods constitute 'ancient woodland' in the officially understood sense that they appear in approximately their present form on the earliest available maps resulting from General Roy's Survey of 1749-55. Deducing

Pl 5.1: Native Scots pine on Glenfinnan Island, praised in 18th century Gaelic poetry

from this, the unwary may underestimate their antiquity. Earlier maps such as that of Blaeu (1654) show the area to be well wooded in the early seventeenth century, and all the evidence of history and the botanical and paleobotanical record points to woodland continuity unbroken since recolonisation after the end of the last Ice Age.

There are now few localities in the Highlands which contain such an extensive area of native broadleaved woodland that has not been disturbed by development. In terms of modern environmental criteria, it is also important because it is relatively free of conifer planting, road construction and other such land-use changes and practices. The only other notable site of such dimension and character beyond this locality is the oak and birch woodland along the north shore of Loch Maree, although direct comparison is not relevant or fair to either habitat.

Gaelic substantives describing wood and trees are the common currency of place-names in the Clanranald mainland territories. Vocabulary is strong in relation to timber and woodland so that words such as *slat* and *sliseag*, used for growing or cut rods or 'wands', are part of everyday speech. In place-names, *coille* 'a wood' is common, and equally common in the Rough Bounds is *doire*, originally meaning a grove or oakwood, occasionally with a mystical association with 'druidical' practice; the word is derived from a putative Indo-European root word *dair* meaning tree and has come to be applied to the oak as the tree par excellence. The names of trees are used to signify the letters of the alphabet in Gaelic, and birch (*beithe*), hazel (*caltuinn*), oak (*darach*), alder (*feàrn*), yew (*iubhar*), and willow (*seileach*), are especially common in place-names in this area.

Tradition is consistent and widespread over the Highlands that woods were once extensive and no longer are so, and that their erosion or even wholesale destruction was due to marching armies or revenge of the conquerors on the conquered. Woods in the Central Highlands, for example, were said to have been burnt on the orders of Mary Queen of Scots to eliminate the hiding places of robbers and political enemies or alternatively the breeding ground of wolves. On the Clanranald mainland territories, it is always said that the forests were reduced by 'the Danes', that is in Gaelic *na Lochlannaich* which is a traditional generic for the Norse invaders. It is believed that Claish Moss at the west end of Loch Sheil, now a National Nature Reserve, was burnt by 'the Danes', which is a rationalisation to explain the presence of large tree trunks and roots in the peat (MacDonald 1889). The balance of evidence is against such explanations of environmental climax and change, but the traditions themselves serve to provide an insight into a symbolic role for woodland in the culture of the Gaelic Highlands (cf. Smith 1797; Wallace 1880-3).

The same rationalisation is evident in Uist tradition in the windswept western periphery of the Clanranald Estates as recorded in the vituperative account of the Outer Hebrides by Rev John Lane Buchanan, who noted impressions gained there between 1782 and 1791 as a missionary with the SPCK:

> However unfavourable this country is to the growth of wood at present, it is evident that there was once great plenty of it all over the islands; for the roots and trunks of large trees are found in deep mosses, bearing unequivocal impressions of fire; which make the people say that the Norwegians burnt the wood when they were obliged to retreat from the Scottish islands and sea coasts to their native Scandinavia. (Buchanan 1793)

In *Heimskringla*, Norse tradition claims that scorched earth was the strategy of attack rather than retreat.

In several western mainland districts, including conspicuously the Rough Bounds of Moidart and Lochaber, it was said that the woods were destroyed by fire in a vengeful act of retaliation or retribution by a witch from Norway. She was the eldest daughter of the king of Norway and was skilled in the 'Black Art' *Sgoil Dubh*. She burnt the woods on the instructions of her father because, it was said, the woods of Lochaber were growing so great as to rival the 'Black Wood of Sweden', *Coille Dhubh na Suain*. Though these traditions seem fanciful, they are instructive. They indicate that the woods were inseparably part of the cultural heritage of the area and that there was an innate understanding of environmental issues since the loss of trees was interpreted as a disaster and an upsetting of the natural order (e.g. Campbell 1895).

Traditions are strong in Moidart and Arisaig that the area was densely wooded, more so even than the surviving relatively extensive natural woods of oak, birch, hazel and ash might suggest. There are one or two circumstantial stories of men and beasts evading pursuit and capture by hiding in woods in areas now comparatively bare of cover. It is evident from sources such as the *Lyon in Mourning*, the manuscript collection of first-hand accounts of the Jacobite campaigns made by the Episcopalian Bishop Robert Forbes, that the woods of the west coast played an important part in sheltering fugitives in the aftermath of the battle of Culloden. Cattle were driven into the woods, and goods and gear were hidden in and under trees. It is not without significance that one of the terms for a state of outlawry was *fo'n choille*, literally 'under the wood' (although it should be added that there are other interpretations of this term). It is still pointed out that when the warships of the Royal Navy were harrying the coasts of Moidart and Arisaig in the summer of 1746, all the cattle of the townships of Glenuig could be hidden beyond detection in a thickly wooded dell at Bealach a' Chara (Gregory 1881; MacDonald 1889; Wood 1950).

We may imagine a continuum of an unchanging climate of life between the Norse invasions and the Highland Clearances. There is little evidence of changes in agricultural practice or regional variation of types of agriculture, although transhumance was very common in this area until the late eighteenth century. Many shieling sites are still evident in the upland core of western Inverness-shire and there are lively traditions concerning their use. When Prince Charles Edward Stuart was in the area after the battle of Culloden, he was fed and sheltered in shieling huts in the hills away from populated areas and lines of communication '...for his accommodation and concealment a few summer shielings or cots could be fitted up amongst the hills..' (Chambers 1869). Change is more readily detectable in social relationships and types of landholding, and the geographical patterns and practices of land management and occupancy in 'pre-improvement' Scotland were in fact extremely varied. One of the elements which was a force for change as well as for stability was the institution of the barony court, which has been inadequately assessed, even hardly mentioned, in relation to woodland history. It has been called by one historian the 'microcosm of rural society and public order', and it determined to a large extent the way in which land was held and managed, and as a consequence affected the nature of change on the land itself (Sanderson 1982). The Clanranald lands were erected into a barony and the chief or his 'baron baillie' presided over his tenants in the baron court and, as well as settling disputes and exercising a power of pit and gallows, regulated agriculture and 'good neighbourhood'. We do not have direct written evidence of the proceedings of a baron court on the Clanranald Estates although the dictates and sanctions of keeping good husbandry and good neighbourhood can be inferred from a number of written tacks and leases. (For examples see SRO 1761; Innes 1855; Campbell 1889-90.)

One of the common elements in the control of land and natural resources in medieval Europe was the 'royal forest' or 'hunting reserve'. Hunting rights and restrictions were a widely exercised form of social control and one of the formulae in the feudal organisation of landholding. The control of hunting in the royal forests extended, depending on population pressure, to the prohibition of woodcutting, grazing of animals, and building. Hunting forests were extensive, demarcated and restrictive by the late thirteenth century but there is no trace in Scotland of the more notorious and vindictive forest laws of England.

Forest was of course a legal rather than an ecological term, recalling the reaction of the native Scot to the Englishman's surprise that he could see no trees in the great deer forests of the north: 'Trees! Wha ever heard tell o trees in a forest?' Forest did not necessarily correspond to woodland and the multiplicity of charters granting rights *in boscis* suggests an investment of power rather than a topographical reference. Nevertheless, restrictions approximating to earlier forest laws appear in later documents such as a group of 'bonds' or contracts between Highland chiefs of the late sixteenth and early seventeenth centuries to ensure the preservation of the habitat of game and the conservation of woodland. The MacDonalds of Clanranald were party to agreements to preserve deer, muirfowl and woodlands in order to keep, as they said, 'guid societie and neighbourhood amongst them' (Iona Club 1847; for an analysis of royal forest see Gilbert 1979).

Coincidentally while the Clanranald chiefs were taking steps to conserve their woodland, they were flexing their political muscles on the Hebridean as well as the national scene and this required manpower, weaponry and ships. These assets are well described in contemporary Gaelic praise poetry which invokes them as the quintessential symbols of power and prestige. Reference is also made to the crafting of them by skilled people, often members of families who served respective chieftains for generations. Research still has to reveal where and when galleys were built. Evidence from a number of sources points to galley building at Kishorn in the sixteenth century, on Loch Awe and Loch Fyne, in Skye and in Barra. They were considered to be one of the most potent threats to peace and the power of the Crown and were made the targets of legislation designed to limit their numbers and size. (A worker in wood, *saer*, was highly regarded in Gaelic society and craftsmen as a class are well represented by inscriptions on funerary monuments. Ship building, like other crafts, was the inherited preserve of a few families such as the *Mac Gille Chonnaill* on Loch Awe, and the *Mac Gille Lùcais* on Loch Fyne who served the Earls of Argyll.) (Gregory 1881; Macphail 1914, 1920).

Evidence of the past can be acquired from a variety of sources. It is most straightforward to read about it but it is more intriguing to be told about it or to deduce it from the survival of relics. There is a vague tradition that the chieftains of Clanranald had their galleys built at Gasgan on Lochsheilside. This location was chosen for its proximity to the best oak woods, possibly the best oak woods on Clanranald's mainland territories, since these woods are rather less accessible to the sea than other coastal woods.

Improving on this, it has been said, in the nature of a conundrum or puzzle, that the chieftains had half their boats built at Gasgan. This conjures up an image of a stem half or stern half of a boat, or a bottom half or a top half of a boat, inviting conjecture on why this sort of exercise should be undertaken. Apparently the explanation lies in the lost arts of galley building in that a shell or skin of planking would be built, perhaps in one location, and subsequently moved to another location for the shaping and fixing of the ribs. In this case, mature oak was preferred for the structural timbers of the

Pl 5.2: Pines on the former Clanranald tack of Arieneskill

galleys and it could be found shaped in natural bends to suit the profile of the hull. It is said that oak was used for the stem and stern posts, keel, ribs and gunwale. Elm was preferred for the strakes (e.g. MacDonald and MacDonald 1924 p 263; cf. Mackay 1919-22).

Material culture has often its own idiom which differs from region to region and locality to locality; it differs according to topography and land forms, coastal and insular locations, climate, population density and economic activity. Thus in detail the material culture of Scotland defies all but the briefest generalisation, since few descriptions apply to more than localities or regions. Descriptions of Highland settlement and cultivation depend for example on accounts of winning peat for fuel, building houses with stone and *fail*, and turning the soil with the *cas chrom* or foot plough. In the Rough Bounds, none of these holds good; fuel was timber, houses often referred to as 'creel houses' were of wood and wattle, and cultivation and arable husbandry, severely limited in area, used the simple 'straight spade' or *cas dhireach*. One of the government factors reporting to the Commissioners of the Forfeited Estates in 1753 wrote:

> The whole houses of the country are made up of twigs manufactured by way of creels called wattling and covered with turff. They are so low in the roof as scarce to admitt a person standing in them, and when these are made up with pains they endure ten or twelve years. They thatch them with rushes (Munro 1984).

Clanranald was careful to control the use of timber, as a tack of 1761 demonstrates: the penny land of Arieneskill (Pl 5.2) was set to three tenants '... upon condition of building houses, making enclosures... with allowance of wood, liberty for building of houses, and other labouring utensils...firr, oak, ash and elm excepted.' (SRO 1761)

Buildings of any size in the Hebrides such as churches and the castle or hall of the chieftains were built of local materials. Evidence is imprecise but suggests that all the roof construction and other timber work used in Castle Tioram in Moidart between the fourteenth and the seventeenth centuries used local oak (MacDonald 1889; Smith 1798). A further intriguing detail points to a crannog site at Arisaig, lived in by a Clanranald chieftain remote in time, and being constructed of oak trees from the slopes above. The derivation of the name 'crannog' is illustrated by the local Gaelic name for it, the *Tigh-chrann* or 'House of Tree Trunks'.

After the Jacobite Rising of 1745-46, about forty estates of those who had been under arms were forfeited as part of the range of important legislation designed to ensure that no further politically motivated force should emerge from the Highlands or Scotland as a whole. The aftermath of the battle of Culloden and the hunting of the fugitive Prince Charles Edward Stuart took less than six months but the consequences of legal sanctions, an army of occupation, and the attrition of Jacobite sympathisers was spread over many years. Under the terms of the Vesting Act of June 1747, it was specified that the estates of those attainted for high treason were to be surveyed and valued so that the rents and profits could be ascertained and made available for the benefit of creditors and the Crown. The administration of these estates was entrusted to the Barons of the Court of Exchequer who were to regard their role as care and maintenance rather than improvement.

A 'Judicial Rental' was prepared inter alia of the Clanranald Estates which in due course were not found liable to forfeiture due to a technical misidentification of the person attainted (MacDonald and MacDonald 1896). In August 1748, David Bruce, as the Surveyor for the Forfeited Estates, toured Clanranald's island and mainland territories examining 'Wadsetters, Tenants and Possessors' and taking sworn statements of the amounts paid by them in cash and kind before 1746, although the real amounts of rents payable may have been concealed. All rentals were expressed in pounds Scots, merks and butter, cheese, 'wedder sheep' or convertible values. The values were low; for example the fourpenny land of Borradale in Arisaig, a substantial tack adjacent to some of the mature natural oakwoods in Glen Beasdale, paid 240 merks which would convert to about £12 sterling. Excepted from the rented property altogether were the woodlands consisting, it was said, of 'oaks, ashes, allers, elm, birch, hazel and several sorts of barren timber' and in August 1748 this was valued, not in Scots money but exceptionally in pounds sterling at £1,000 (SRO E.744/1/70; cf. E.764/14/4 Exchequer Papers). This reflects the high regard for the woods of the proprietor; the valuers were local men, Aeneas MacDonald of Dalilea and Donald MacVarish of Annat.

More or less contemporary with the Judicial Rental is the poetry of the Clanranald bard and greatest of all Gaelic poets, Alexander MacDonald. In his 'Salute to Morar' he praises all the mainland territories of Clanranald for their fertility, abundance of cattle and their luxuriant woodlands, trees being

Pl 5.3: Mature oakwoods on Loch Moidart

an essential element of this natural wealth. The long poem is rich in hyperbole, but this cannot be dismissed as such. It is part of a panegyric code of long ancestry in which the landscape becomes a rhetorical device to reflect the rule of the just and generous leader. Terms such as 'woods' and 'trees', along with 'fruits' and 'berries' are full of emotional energy and provide the appropriate imagery of a rich countryside (MacDonald and MacDonald 1924 pp. 36-43). Woods provide a significant toponymic metaphor in local district names such as *Suaineart ghorm an daraich* 'green Sunart of the oak trees', *Arasaig Dubh-Ghorm a' Bharraich* 'Blue-black Arisaig of the Woodlands', and *Cnoideart a' Bharraich* 'Knoydart of the Woodlands'.

A further survey of the Clanranald Estates was made in 1798 after the unexpected death of the chieftain in 1794 left his son as a minor. The Judicial Rental reflects contemporary rises in prices and land values following the outbreak of the Napoleonic Wars (SRO 1798a). Rents expressed in pounds sterling were high, rent in kind was no longer assessed, and express reference is made under each township to the amount of kelp made annually. The township of Mingarry in the hands of five tenants paid £30 sterling, having paid about £6 sterling in 1748 divided between six tenants paying varying sums in pounds Scots, merks and casualties. The small coastal township of Egnaig under two tenants and making 26cwt of kelp paid £43, but had paid only 32 pounds Scots in 1748 (about £3 sterling). The woodlands escaped valuation because they had already substantially been disposed of to the Lorne Furnace Company. Excepted from the sale in December 1794 had been '... the patch of Blackwood in Braeborodale in the Glen betwixt Marmy and Arnapull on the farm of Dalilea in Moydart' (SRO 1794). Two tenants were appointed Clanranald's woodkeepers in Arisaig and Moidart respectively, one at a salary of £10. In addition, allowances were made in the rents of three tenants for 'grounds, enclosed and planted' and 'preservation of woods' (SRO 1798b).

Most of the factors affecting the Highlands as a whole in the late eighteenth century are detectable in the same critical forms on the Clanranald Estates. Opinion favoured a populous countryside in the prevailing intellectual climate of improving ideology. There was some optimism for the development of agriculture and a fishing industry in the Highlands, and kelping provided employment for as many people as could be found. A rise in population increased the pressure on resources, in some years to famine conditions, especially for example in 1772-3 when it was reported of the west coast that:

> ... the Poor People... are in a most pitiable situation for want of Meal. They are reduced to live on Blood which they draw from their Cattle by repeated Bleedings. Need we wonder to hear of Emigrations from such a Country (*Aberdeen Journal* 13 September 1773; cf. SRO Gordon Castle Muniments).

There was surprise and shock over tacksman-led emigration from the Clanranald Estates in 1772 that induced 200 to leave the island and mainland properties, apparently on religious grounds rather than in search of economic betterment. But the economic imperative was still a powerful one for the chieftain and tacksmen. The rise in prices in the second half of the eighteenth century, accelerated by the outbreak of the Napoleonic Wars, brought a rise in land values and rises in rents. Cash from the sale of cattle now became available in greater measure from sheep rearing. New breeds of sheep were introduced into the Clanranald mainland properties in the 1780s and the *Statistical Account* of the district written in 1795 catalogues the enormity of arguably the greatest change ever experienced by the region. The voice of the people was raised in protest against this as contemporary Gaelic song has preserved it. The traditional balance of the old animal husbandry was 1,151 cattle and 1,000 sheep, but a massive influx of 11,750 sheep of 'the better sort', that is the larger, coarse wool, black-faced sheep swamped the local economy (Campbell 1798; cf 'Lament for the Laird of Glenaladale').

This transformation of Moidart and Arisaig into a short-term productive source of cheap wool and meat for urbanising and industrialising Britain was rapid and devastating. Little or no heed was now given to the protection of woodlands, and the marginal uses to which it was put were of less consequence to the landlord. A regime of continuous muirburn and deforestation was introduced. Small-scale local iron smelting declined and boat-building gave way to unskilled boat-repairing. Timber was sold to the companies operating at centres such as Bonawe in the mid-eighteenth century, although Clanranald's woods were almost beyond practicable reach for them (e.g. SRO Articles anent the Sale of Clanranald's Woods). The company smelting at Bonawe from 1753 had tacks of woods in the area and may have taken timber from the south shore of Loch Sheil (e.g. Lindsay 1975). Although the records are not clear it seems likely that they thoroughly cleared an area known as *Leitir Seile* of its mature timber in this period. Charcoal burning mounds can be traced in the Clanranald woods themselves (Fig 5.5). Glenfinnan was a source for charcoal collection between 1796 and 1801, when timber and charcoal were transported up the loch and then overland and by sea through Loch Eil to Bonawe, prompting the plan to cut a canal between the head of Loch Sheil and Kinlocheil.

Oral tradition suggests in a subtle and telling change of emphasis that the woods served only to hide and to fuel the considerable local industry of illicit distilling in its dispersed locations; it was comparatively efficient in this area whose arable economy was minimal but attracted barley and mash from as far away as Tiree to be converted into a portable commodity and a rent in kind (Cameron 1957).

The physical resources and wildlife in the region are of national and international importance, a judgement formed by modern standards of nature conservation and one which we would applaud. This rich woodland and its wildlife habitats that have survived are an essential element in the biological diversity whose preservation for future generations is now our pledge.

Understanding the natural environment is one of the means of effective preservation and it is easier to devise a strategy of protection and conservation when we have a more intimate knowledge of the landscape and its history beyond assumptions and generalisations. Historical analysis

Pl 5.4: Pine and birch woods between Moidart and Arisaig that escaped late
18th century destruction

suggests, therefore, that the degrading of landscape in the Clanranald
territories has been short rather than long term and should be more easily
reversible. In addition, the natural forest cover may never have been as
extensive as we like to imagine. The verdict of Cosmo Innes, nineteenth
century lawyer and prolific record scholar, was cautious but as timeous today
as it was when published in 1837. He commented 'on the common belief that
Scotland was anciently thickly covered with wood' and wrote: 'If it ever
were so, it must have been at a time beyond all record' (Innes 1837 xv,
1861).

Bibliography

Anderson M L 1967. *A History of Scottish Forestry*. Edinburgh
Buchanan J L 1793. *Travels in the Western Hebrides from 1782 to 1790*. London
Cameron A 1957. *St Finan's Isle, Eilean Fhianain*. Oban
Campbell A 1798. Parish of Ardnamurchan. *Statistical Account* Vol. XX
Campbell D 1889-90. Baron Bailie Court at Balrobert, Inverness, 1677. *The Highland
    Monthly* I: 468-71
Campbell J G 1895. Clan Traditions and Popular Tales. In: *Waifs and Strays of Celtic*

Tradition. Vol. V: Argyllshire Series. London

Carruthers R 1843. *The Highland Note-Book*. Edinburgh

Chambers R 1869. *History of the Rebellion of 1745-6*. 7th edn. Edinburgh

Darling F Fraser 1947. *Natural History in the Highlands and Islands*. Collins, London

Darling F Fraser (ed.) 1955. *West Highland Survey*. Oxford University Press, Oxford

Gilbert J M 1979. *Hunting and Hunting Reserves in Medieval Scotland*. John Dondald, Edinburgh (pp.234-39 describe measures taken at law to protect growing timber such as fines imposed by act of parliament on 'stealers of green wood and bark peelers' as early as 1424)

Gregory D 1881. *The History of the Western Highlands and Isles of Scotland from AD 1493 to AD 1625*. 2nd edn. London

Innes C (ed.) 1837. *Liber Sancte Marie de Melros*. Vol. 1. Bannatyne Club, Edinburgh

Innes C (ed.) 1855. *The Black Book of Taymouth*. Bannatyne Club, Edinburgh

Innes C 1861. *Sketches of Early Scotch History*. Edinburgh

Iona Club 1847. *Collectanea de Rebus Albanicis*.

'Lament for the Laird of Glenaladale' In: *Orain le Raoghall Donullach an Ardnis, Arasaig*. 1821. Inbhirnis

Lindsay J M 1975. Charcoal iron-smelting and its fuel-supply: the example of Lorn Furnace, Argyllshire 1753-1876. *Journal of Historical Geography* 1: 283-98

MacDonald A, MacDonald A 1896. *The Clan Donald*. Vol. 1. Inverness

MacDonald A, MacDonald A 1924. *The Poems of Alexander Macdonald (Mac Mhaighstir Alasdair)*. Inverness

MacDonald C 1889. *Moidart or Among the Clanranalds*. Oban

Mackay J G 1919-22. Social Life in Skye from Legend and Story Pt. III. *Trans. of the Gaelic Society of Inverness* 30

Macphail J R N (ed.) 1914. *Highland Papers Volume I*. Scottish History Society

Macphail J R N (ed.) 1920. *Highland Papers Volume III*. Scottish History Society

Munro R W 1984. *Taming the Rough Bounds. Knoydart 1745-1784*. Society of West Highland and Island Historical Research

Sanderson M H B 1982. *Scottish Rural Society in the Sixteenth Century*. John Donald, Edinburgh

SRO 1761. Tack for 10 years to the tenants of Arieniskill, Arisaig. Scottish Record Office GD 201/2/28

SRO 1794. Contract of Wood between the Commissioners of John MacDonald Esquire and the Lorn Furnace Company, 1 and 2 December 1794. Scottish Record Office GD 201/5/204

SRO 1798a. Notarial Copy of the Judicial Rental of Clanranald's Estate, 2 October 1798. Scottish Record Office GD 201/5/216

SRO 1798b. Notarial Copy of the Judicial Rental of Clanranald's Estate, 2 October 1798. Scottish Record Office GD 201/5/216/113, 150

SRO Gordon Castle Muniments. Scottish Record Office GD 44/27/11

SRO Articles anent the Sale of Clanranald's Woods. Scottish Record Office GD 201/1/359/2

Smith J 1797. Parish of Campbeltown. *Statistical Account*. Vol. X

Smith J 1798. *General View of the Agriculture of the County of Argyll*. Edinburgh

Steven H M, Carlisle A 1959. *The Native Pinewoods of Scotland*. Oliver & Boyd, Edinburgh

Wallace T D 1880-83. Archaeological Notes. *Transactions of the Inverness Scientific Society* II: 314

Wood W 1950. *Moidart and Morar*. Edinburgh

6

MARGINAL AGRICULTURE IN SCOTLAND

Stratford P Halliday

The words 'marginal agriculture' appear to convey a readily understood concept. After all, margins are edges, carrying with them implications of centres or cores, so there can be little doubt that this chapter is concerned with agriculture at the edges. But what are these edges? How can they be defined? How can we recognise them? And can the space that they occupy shift through time? Even in terms of modern agriculture, these apparently simple questions obscure numerous complex issues, but for past societies there is the additional problem of their remoteness in time. Man has been farming the Scottish landscape for at least six thousand years, and our understanding of how he lived is only as detailed as the scraps of surviving evidence allow. Environmental historians can now show that the landscape has been in a continuous process of change within that period, and pollen grains preserved in peat deposits allow the developments of local environments to be charted in some detail. Although the timing of the various stages of development may differ widely from area to area, they usually conform to a broad pattern. Initially there is evidence of clearings in the natural forest, both opening and closing, but invariably there comes a point when the clearings expand dramatically and the forest never recovers. A crude caricature, but, when coupled with the telltale signs of agriculture that accompany many of the changes, one that charts the arrival of the first farmers and the progressive development of Scotland's agricultural economy. The first part of this chapter briefly discusses marginality, before going on to examine and interpret some of the traces of agriculture that can be recovered by archaeological fieldwork.

In many ways marginality is a modern concept, its purpose the explanation of observation, rather than the observation itself. And yet, flicking through the pages of an agricultural atlas of Scotland (Coppock 1976), one is left in little doubt that the margins are real and exist. The distribution of rough pasture, for instance, with its heavy preponderance in the uplands, coupled with the extent of tillage (Coppock 1976, pp. 45, 50), appears to make a very bold statement about agricultural marginality. But the margins are much more complex than this, as an examination of the different types of production clearly shows. Each type, be it arable or pastoral, has a core area and a periphery. To this more complex pattern must then be added the distance to markets and the concentrations of population that these generally imply.

At once, it is apparent that the agricultural margins are relative zones, varying with each crop or product. Leaving aside the question of marketing, the clue to a farmers success, both today and in the past, must lie in the selection of the crops or animals that are appropriate to his local environment. If his choice is inappropriate, at best it will cost a larger investment of resources for him to succeed, at worst he will not only make the investment but also fail. This, of course, is the fundamental point with regard to past farming communities; while they might be able to sustain the loss of one crop, failure in two successive years would spell disaster.

Most of the rural communities that date from before the industrialisation of agriculture and the growth of the urban population were probably dependent on a mixed economy. Indeed, it is only with the rise of large population centres that farmers have become specialised in certain types of production, usually with a view to maximising their profits within a money-based economy. Such centres were probably in existence in some parts of Scotland by the Late Bronze Age (ca.1000BC), although a money-based economy first arrived with the Roman army a millennium later. Even with the existence of such centres throughout Scotland, it is likely that each rural community had to be largely self-sufficient, and it is probable that the proportions of different produce of each community were broadly reflected in the proportions of land made over to each type of production on each farm. This is of course a sweeping generalisation which cannot be proven for the prehistoric period, but, equally, it would have been the only form of insurance policy available to early farmers. Specialisation was to risk disaster for the individual farmer and his family: generalisation, however, risked disaster for the entire community in a particularly inclement season.

Today there is a bewildering array of different crops, each with a multitude of specially-bred strains, and all of them designed to help the farmer succeed. Research has enabled drought-resistance and other hardy characteristics to be bred into many crops. This work has provided modern farmers with crop-varieties that can be cultivated with less risk of failure in marginal environments. Socio-political expediency has also sustained some of the costs of production. Previous generations of farmers had a much narrower choice of crops upon which to mix their economy, and their successes or failures must have been closely tied to unseasonal fluctuations in the weather.

Climate is clearly the most influential factor that constrains the cultivation of crops, and is therefore the major factor defining the zones where certain types of agricultural production might be considered marginal. Therefore, the extent of any marginal zone can only have remained constant for as long as the climate was in some form of equilibrium. Research, however, has shown that the climate is in a continuous state of change, with both long-term trends and short-term fluctuations (Ch.1 this volume). Thus, it is possible to answer one of the questions raised in the first paragraph; the extent of any marginal zone defined in agricultural terms must change with the fluctuations of the climate. In the past, farming communities must have been far more vulnerable to the impact of climatic changes, particularly at times when the demands of a large population was forcing farmers into less and less advantageous locations. For this reason there has been considerable interest in archaeological circles concerning the impact of climatic change on early settlement in Scotland.

The problems of defining marginality have been extensively discussed by Martin Parry (1985). In the Lammermuirs, he has mapped the theoretical limits of cereal cultivation during the medieval period in terms of accumulated temperature and potential water surplus. The zones defined are by no means absolute, but they do illustrate the potential impact of climatic change in the uplands. He has also gone on to suggest that by mapping the theoretical limits of cereal cultivation at past extremes of climatic fluctuation, it is possible to identify a recurrently marginal zone. His data was collected for the medieval period, and extended across the whole of the British Isles on the basis of accumulated temperature, taking no account of the potential water surplus and exposure, which would influence the pattern at regional and local levels. In general terms, the pattern that might be anticipated for earlier periods would be broadly similar.

In terms of the archaeology of agriculture, Parry's map of the recurrently marginal zone has a wider application. In effect, he has approximately mapped the zone through which agriculture has ebbed and flowed, not only during the medieval period, but also over a wide span of prehistory. At times

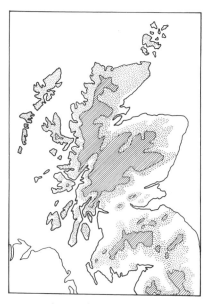

Fig 6.1: Map showing recurrently marginal (stippled) and sub-marginal (hatched) areas in Scotland (after Parry 1985)

when the population has increased, the demands on agriculture have also increased, forcing farmers on to the more marginal locations. Each time arable agriculture has been forced across this zone it has erased some of the evidence of earlier episodes of cultivation. Thus, the surviving archaeological remains of cultivation systems of any period, either prehistoric or medieval, are always found beyond the edges of cultivation remains of the succeeding periods. The recurrently marginal zone defines the area within which traces of every period of agricultural expansion are potentially recoverable by fieldwork, although in practice the pattern of survival is more complex than this; modern improved agriculture has often swept this zone bare, but close examination of many of the surviving sites often reveals a jumbled mass of remains from widely differing periods. In effect, successive expansions of agriculture, culminating in the Improvements of the late eighteenth and nineteenth century, have marginalised the upstanding remains of prehistoric and medieval field-systems, only allowing them to survive in areas which are now either marginal or else virtually unusable for arable crops. It should also be remembered that these locations have also suffered from six thousand years of environmental attrition, particularly deforestation and soil-degradation.

The archaeology of the Neolithic provides a dramatic example of how agriculture has marginalised the majority of the upstanding archaeological monuments of every period. The principal monuments to survive from the Neolithic are chambered tombs and long mounds, but for much of Scotland these are situated in open moorland in apparently remote locations. This case has become glaringly obvious from the work that the Royal Commission on the Ancient and Historical Monuments of Scotland has been doing in South-east Perth and on the Braes of Doune. The Braes of Doune survey, carried out by the Afforestable Land Survey, has produced no less than three examples of chambered tombs and one long cairn, and there is now a marked concentration of Neolithic burial-mounds in the hills of western Perthshire; but, looking north-eastwards across South-east Perth and up Strathmore, out across some of the richest agricultural land of Scotland, there is not another Neolithic burial-monument to be seen for fifty miles. Are we seriously to suppose that Neolithic farmers ignored the greater part of eastern Scotland? No, of course not, and the distributions of artefacts such as stone axes, and the cropmarks of early prehistoric ceremonial monuments, clearly reveal his presence. Ironically, these forms of evidence can only be collected in areas which are under cultivation, the very areas where the majority of the upstanding evidence has been removed.

This idea of an archaeological margin, which is perhaps best defined as a zone of survival rather than preservation, is not simply the preserve of Neolithic monuments. The pattern of survival of each period throughout prehistory and history has been shaped by the succeeding episodes of agricultural exploitation, culminating in the reorganisation of the landscape during the Improvements. Neolithic remains have been removed in the Early Bronze Age, whose remains have been removed in their turn by Late Bronze Age settlement and agriculture. So the process has gone on through six millennia and is as relevant to the post-medieval period as it is to the prehistoric. The pre-crofting landscape of Skye, for instance, is as much a product of this process as the swathes of stone clearance heaps that have been recorded in North-east Perth (RCAHMS 1990). All the upstanding remains of agriculture for every period must be drawn from this margin, but the local variations in patterns of settlement, coupled with patterns of environmental change, have created an unnatural selection in which each area of Scotland only has a limited range of the total available evidence. Thus, anyone wanting to study the physical remains of Neolithic fields must go to Shetland (as far as is currently known). But, we have no idea whether the fields surviving in Shetland are an expression of Neolithic agricultural in what was, even then, a marginal environment, or whether they represent the norm that once existed in forest clearings over the whole of Scotland. The evidence of peat ash spread across the fields at Scord of Brouster in Shetland (Whittle 1986), and also at a slightly later date in some of the machair sites of the outer isles, speaks of an empirical knowledge of soil fertility and the benefits of manuring, which must have been the stock in trade of all Neolithic farmers, but the only possible traces of a Neolithic field from eastern Scotland are the traces of cultivation ridges discovered by excavation beneath a large round barrow at Strathallan in Perthshire (Barclay 1990).

In fact, the absence of Neolithic fields from the rest of Scotland may be more apparent than real. The basic components of the Scord of Brouster field-system—the clearance heaps, the stony banks and the low lynchets—are all features that turn up around prehistoric settlements elsewhere. What is much rarer, and may well be the case on Shetland too, is to find fields with four sides. Even where they do apparently exist they should be treated with caution; excavation at An Sithean on Islay showed that three sides of one 'field' were all of different dates (Barber and Brown 1985). Indeed, one of the major lessons of excavation on hut-circle groups and their attendant agricultural remains has been to show that such sites are seldom the result of one period of occupation, with evidence of successive episodes of use spread over several millennia.

The work that has recently been completed by RCAHMS in North-east Perth (1990) provides a good case-study for the various types of remains that survive in the Highland landscape, and the problems of interpretation that they pose. Examination of the prehistoric settlements shows that there is no standard set of agricultural remains around any of the distinctive types of hut-circle that exist in the area. The double-walled hut-circles, for instance, can be found in isolation, amongst scatters of clearance heaps, some with occasional stony banks, and in very formal arrangements of field-banks, with in one case, Drumturn Burn, recognisable fields. The latter, however, is virtually unique in the area, and, while it undoubtedly represents a complex set of agricultural practices, there is no evidence to suggest that the same set of practices has been in use on any other site in the area. Thus, although the Drumturn Burn field-system may be of considerable interest in itself, it cannot be used to explain how the rest of the landscape in North-east Perth was being farmed in prehistory.

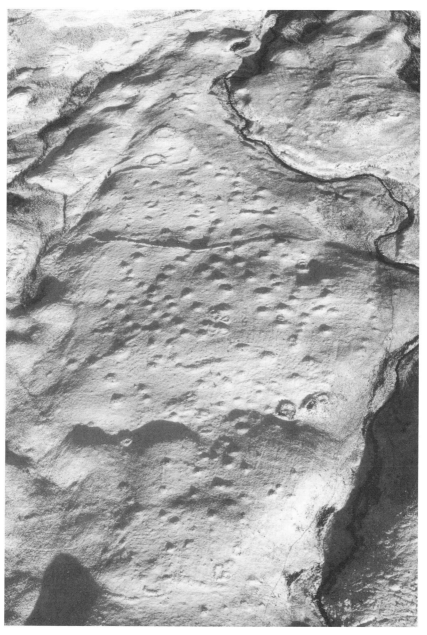

Pl 6.1: Pitcarmick Burn, North-east Perth: aerial photograph showing a scatter of clearance heaps along a low moorland ridge, with two hut-circles visible at the upper end. Faint traces of later cultivation ridges can be detected amongst the cairns, and also a number of rectangular shieling huts (courtesy of RCAHMS).

The problems of transposing the evidence from sites such as Drumturn Burn to other locations encapsulates the whole problem of interpreting this form of evidence. The problem can only be resolved by returning to the excavated evidence which consistently shows that these Highland sites have been used on numerous separate occasions. Our explanations must be conceived in terms of multiperiod models, which allow the successive modification of the surviving remains as settlement has expanded and contracted. It is also important to see the whole landscape as a multiperiod archaeological site, and to look at the problem posed by a hillside that has already been used on several occasions over the preceding millennia from the point of view of a prehistoric farmer. He has a simple problem: on the one hand, a finite labour resource, and on the other, a minimum essential return, without which his family will not be able to survive to repeat the cycle the following year. If his hillside is apparently virgin, he can lay out fields and whatever else he requires to his hearts content, perhaps producing a prehistoric equivalent of some rather twee small-holding. But if his hillside is already dotted with clearance heaps, old banks and derelict hut-circles, he must ask himself whether the input required to clear the hillside and lay out his ideal farm will be justified by the returns. He has a straight question of value for money. In later periods, there are glimpses of the same question, which is implicit in the occurrence of later cultivation ridges overlying the fields at Drumturn Burn and also in amongst the clearance heaps on many other hillsides in North-east Perth. In one case in Wigtownshire, at Kilhern, where the remains of an earlier clearance system have been subsumed into a rig-system, the later farmer has even dug lazy-beds across the interior of a hut-circle but not cleared away its wall. Perhaps, this sort of evidence is providing a clue to a possible definition of marginal farming in the prehistoric period; it is farming in environments where the potential yields only justify the minimum inputs of labour into clearing stones and other built obstructions. Looking back into North-east Perth it becomes possible to understand why there is such a variation in the agricultural remains around the double-walled hut-circles; Drumturn Burn was either laid out on a virgin hillside, or the potential return justified the removal of any earlier scatter of structures that may have existed there. At other groups of hut-circles, lying amongst simple scatters of cairns, this was clearly not the case.

Unlike the hut-circles of North-east Perth, those in the rest of the Highlands, and down the western seaboard into Galloway, tend to form a monoculture of stony rings, notable exceptions occurring in parts of Sutherland and Grampian. The agricultural remains that are found around them are much the same as in North-east Perth, dominated by clusters of scrappy clearance heaps, but occasionally accompanied by simple enclosures or more extensive systems of field-banks. Similar remains of agricultural clearance are relatively rare in south-eastern Scotland, although extensive groups of small cairns have been recorded in Lanarkshire. On the Border hills, however, there is a growing body of agricultural evidence of a rather different character, which allows some of the prehistoric cultivation practices to be explored in greater detail. This is the evidence provided by cord rig.

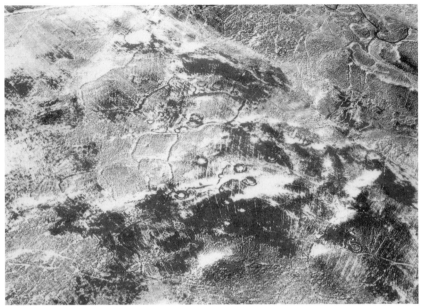

Pl 6.2: Drumturn Burn, North-east Perth: aerial view of a large hut-circle group and its surrounding fields. Later cultivation ridges overlie the field-system
(courtesy of RCAHMS)

Unlike clearance heaps and stony banks, a plot of cord rig actually is a field, whose definition, to quote the dictionary, is simply 'a piece of ground appropriated to pasture or tillage, usually parted off by hedges, fences, boundary stones etc'. The cord rig represents the prehistoric treatment of the soil of a field, a field, furthermore, which rarely has any trace of enclosing boundaries. While the clearance cairns and banks that are so common in the Highlands are relatively static objects in the landscape, tending to survive from one period of use to another, the extent and layout of a plot of cord rig were dynamic, changing with every season of cultivation.

The evidence for how these plots of ridging were cultivated is ambiguous. A section dug at Hut Knowe North in the Cheviots apparently revealed steep-sided furrows that could only have been produced with spades, but a second section on the same site, and another on Orchard Rig in Peeblesshire, showed a much slighter furrow. Three features that have been noted on cord-rig systems suggest that hand implements played a major part in the process of cultivation of the plots: the first of these is the presence of large stones sticking up through some of the ridges; the second is the complete absence of any headlands where fields of rig block together at right-angles to each other; and the third is the way the rigs sometimes split in two to fill awkward corners in a system. In the lowlands of Northumberland, however, excavation of the cord rig beneath the Roman fort at Rudchester (Gillam, Harrison and Newman 1973) and the temporary camp at Greenlea Lough has revealed palimpsests of ard-marks in the subsoil, and there is no evidence for the use of any other type of tool at either site. The two sources of information are not irreconcilable, because there is also evidence from the Cheviots of cultivation which has simply produced a smoothed surface. Indeed, most of the plots of cord rig that have been recorded exist within a larger area of smoothing. By inference the episode of smoothing must predate the ridging, but there is also evidence from both Scowther Knowe and Camp Tops in the Cheviots of smooth areas edged by cultivation scars which cut through plots of cord rig. It is likely that the two forms of surface—the ridging and the smoothing—are different stages in the same agricultural cycle. The smooth areas may well have been created by ploughing, while the ridges were probably only produced once a tilth had been formed. A long-handled hoe or mattock would be a suitable tool for the job, and would probably also account for the narrow gauge of the rigs.

The smoothed areas in the Cheviots have also provided a deeper insight into the way forest was cleared, and settlement expanded into new locations. The evidence is largely derived from the ground surfaces that surround the smoothed areas, for these are often rough and pitted. At several places it is possible to detect traces of the pitted surfaces beneath areas of smoothing and ridging. Detailed examination of some of the pitted surfaces has shown

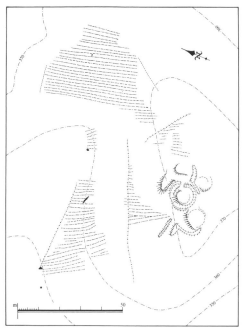

Fig 6.2: Scowther Knowe, Cheviots: plan of a timber-built settlement of ring-ditch houses with adjacent plots of cord rig. Two of the plots to the north of the settlement are clearly cut by cultivation scars marking the edges of smoothed areas. Stones poking through the rigs have been blacked in.

that the pits are accompanied by minor semi-circular grooves and low mounds of upcast. All these features can be paralleled in old forestry plantations, where the trees have blown over and the stumps long since rotted away. The rough and pitted surfaces are almost certainly physical evidence of the prehistoric forest which once clothed the Border hills but is usually only known from pollen diagrams. Far from having been felled by axes, the natural forest on the crests of the hills apparently blew over and failed to regenerate, leaving traces of tree-throws from the Cheviots right up to the Pentlands. The fact that trees should be blowing over is of little significance in itself. This is all part of the forest cycle. But, the lack of regeneration is surely of some significance. In the normal course of events, fallen trees create the spaces in the forest canopy for young saplings to grow up. The only factor that can prevent regeneration is intensive browsing. If the forest has dwindled to a few stands of trees this might be effected by wild animals, but the scale upon which it appears to have taken place on the Border hills strongly suggests concentrated and prolonged grazing, the most likely culprits being herds and flocks of domesticated animals. Here then is the insidious process of man's clearance of the natural forest for agriculture in action.

The complete absence of windblown tree-throws distorting the interiors or perimeters of any of the numerous prehistoric settlements in the Border counties suggests that many of the hilltops had been cleared in this way by a relatively early date. The detailed chronology of these sites is still uncertain but they probably span the greater part of the first millennium BC. Some, however, would have required massive quantities of timber for their construction, so it can hardly be argued that the forest cover had been entirely stripped from the hills by this time. In all probability we are looking at the evidence of hill pastures, probably maintained by seasonal grazing patterns rather than permanent occupation. But why the crests of the ridges, which tend to be the most exposed locations, rather than valley-sides? To be fair, the subsequent arable exploitation of the valleys may have removed similar evidence from the more sheltered spots. Nevertheless, it is worth remembering that the ridges have traditionally provided the route-ways, as is attested by the numerous hollow trackways that survive today. It is only relatively recently that the valleys have become the principal routes through and into the hills. It is not unreasonable to suggest that a transhuming population from the neighbouring lowlands would first exploit the ground along the natural routeways, before descending into the less accessible parts of the valleys.

What is also particularly noticeable in the Cheviots is that the distribution of timber-built settlements—palisades and large round houses—also tends to be concentrated on the crests of the hills, although there is again the possibility that similar sites have been destroyed on the lower slopes. These settlements presumably represent an expansion of permanent settlement out of the adjacent lowlands and probably date to the period between 800BC and 500BC. That they should turn up on the areas that I have argued are hill pastures is surely no coincidence. What could be more natural than to set out

Pl 6.3: Woden Law, Cheviots: aerial photograph of a palisaded settlement with traces of internal timber houses and surrounding cord rig picked out by the snow. (courtesy of D W Harding)

Pl 6.4: Gray Coat, Cheviots: aerial photograph, under snow, of a large circular house enclosed by twin palisades, with traces of a second house at the top of the picture and cord rig in between. (courtesy of RCAHMS)

the new settlements on traditional pastures rather than converting areas of virgin forest into fields. After all this is much the same process that has left a series of modern farms in the Borders with shieling place-names, signifying the origin of the farm on ground previously used for transhumance pasture. In the case of the timber-built settlements, this period of expansion cannot have been particularly long-lived, since many display only one period of use prior to desertion. This is not to say that these upland locations were completely abandoned again; several of the settlements provide evidence of successive buildings and perimeters, and in some cases the timber perimeters have been replaced by stone walls or earthworks.

Detailed study of the cord-rig systems has revealed other evidence of elements of the agricultural cycle that is simply not available from the survey of clusters of clearance heaps. A section cut across some of the rigs at Hut Knowe North, in the Cheviots, suggested that they had been refurbished at some time; when the state of preservation of individual rigs was assessed in the course of the survey, it emerged that a roughly rectangular plot of prominent rigs could be identified at this point, aligned with the furrows of a much fainter set of rigs immediately downslope. Apparently one set of rigs had been superimposed directly on another. The relative state of preservation within each system, on a scale ranging from prominent to barely visible, provides a rough guide as to which were last cultivated on that site, an observation which can be transposed to other sites with interesting results. At Hut Knowe East, for instance, where there is a remarkable pattern of fields defined by low banks, the state of preservation changes from field to field. If the fields with prominent rigs were cultivated in the final season before abandonment, it is hard to escape the conclusion that those with only faint traces were probably lying fallow at the same time. If this is the case, then by the end of the first millennium BC at least one farmer in the Borders must have been practising some form of crop rotation.

This sort of evidence suggests that prehistoric farmers were exploiting large areas of the Border landscape with complex and sophisticated agricultural systems by the first millennium BC. It is worth noting, however, that the majority of cord-rig systems are very small and cannot have provided much more than a supplement to a community's diet. In the hills, at least, the emphasis of the mixed farms must surely have rested on pasture and livestock. Indeed, there is virtually no evidence of arable agriculture around any of the succeeding forts and settlements that crowned the hills until the end of the first millennium BC. Then, the valley sides were opened up by a rash of small farming units, some of which appear to have surviving field-systems on a par with that on Hut Knowe East.

These complex patterns of land-use cannot have been unique to the Borders and there is no reason why similar practices were not in use in the north and west of Scotland. The cord rig is now beginning to turn up in areas where the hills are masked by peat and it is only a matter of time before the complete range of evidence that can be found in the Borders is revealed elsewhere. At Lairg, in Sutherland (*Current Archaeology* 131 [1992]: 455-9) and on Arran (*ibid* 83 [1982]: 359-63) extensive cord-rig systems have been

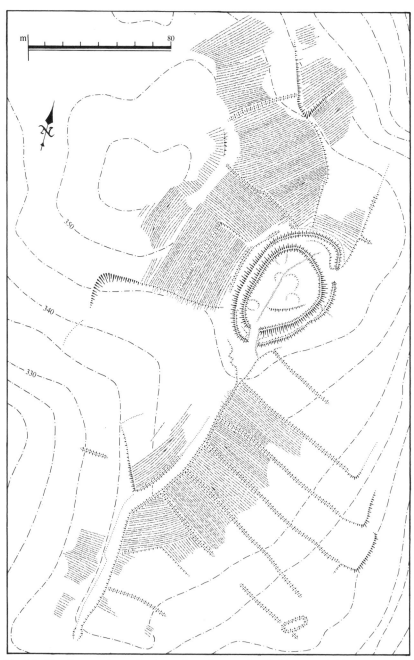

Fig 6.3: Hut Knowe East, Cheviots: plan of a complex field-system laid out along a trackway leading up to the settlement.

recorded beneath the peat and excavation has revealed very similar patterns to those inferred by survey in the Cheviots. The apparent absence of stock-proof enclosures amongst the field-systems of the north and west is as striking as their absence from the majority of cord-rig systems, but there is no particular requirement for fenced enclosures in a system where the arable component is kept close to home and the sheep and cattle are moved off to distant pastures at the crucial seasons when the crops are growing and ripening. The ragged groups of clearance heaps of the Highlands would fit quite happily into this sort of system, although the complete absence of domestic structures from the majority of examples perhaps suggests other complexities to the agricultural system. Some groups of small cairns may represent the improvement of the pasture and were only brought into cultivation with the expansion of settlement; others are perhaps outfields, cropped in rotation to supplement the main sources of cultivated food.

Somewhere in this equation must lie the concept of marginality, but the evidence from the Borders certainly obscures its significance. As long as the hills were used for transhumance pasture, they were not marginal within the terms of that agricultural system. It is only when the agricultural basis for farming the hills apparently changes at about 800BC that the hills become marginal. Presumably the rash of abandoned timber-built settlements on the hills reflects an inappropriate choice of agricultural produce and technique. The expansion of arable farming on to the hills at the end of the first millennium BC was perhaps more successful, but ultimately it was to suffer the same fate, as was the expansion of medieval cultivation over a millennium later. Again the hills reverted to pasture, providing a suitable environment for the Cheviot sheep to thrive.

But why was settlement expanding in the Borders at the beginning of the first millennium BC, at a time when man was rapidly retreating from the hinterland of so many other areas in northern and western Scotland? Marginality is being seen as the key to understanding events in the north and west, where the effects of the eruption of Hekla III on Iceland at the end of the second millennium BC is being seen as a trigger for the desertion of the hut-circle settlements across vast swathes of country. Apparently this event had relatively little impact in the Borders, perhaps reflecting how any concept of the agricultural margin must be adapted to a specific range of products. In the north and west, a dependence on arable crops may not have been sustainable in the face of extreme climatic fluctuations triggered by Hekla III, but the economic base in the south-east, which had a considerably drier climate in any case, was possibly rather different. The same range of techniques were available, but the emphasis of the mixed economy may not have rested so heavily on arable production. The margin of the Border farmers was differently drawn, and far less affected.

The evidence to support the picture presented here tends to be fairly circumstantial. The straws from which past farming systems are reconstructed will always remain elusive, but what has emerged is that man's farming activities were not limited to the immediate environs of the built settlements that we can identify. He was exploiting the landscape in the broadest sense of the word, and while some of his activities have left a major mark, others are rather more fleeting in their appearance, or perhaps even invisible. Furthermore, the same processes that have marginalised so much of the physical evidence for agriculture are also responsible for marginalising our natural wildernesses. Natural wildernesses are our perception of modern environments. Some are undoubtedly man-made wastes today, and few can have entirely escaped prehistoric man's attention. Witness the broken Neolithic bow (now in the National Museum of Scotland) found in a peat bog at a height of about 600m OD in the Southern Uplands, on the watershed between the tributaries of the Tweed and the Annan.

Bibliography

Barber J, Brown M M 1985. An Sithean, Islay. *Proc Soc Antiq Scot,* 114 (1984): 161-88
Barclay G J 1990. The cultivation remains beneath the North Mains, Strathallan, barrow. *Proc Soc Antiq Scot,* 119 (1989): 59-61
Coppock J T 1976. *An Agricultural Atlas of Scotland.* John Donald, Edinburgh
Gillam J P, Harrison R M, Newman T G 1973. Interim report on the excavations at Rudchester 1972. *Arch Aeliana,* 5th series, 1: 81-5
Parry M L 1985. Upland Settlement and Climatic Change: the Medieval Evidence. In: Spratt D, Burgess C (eds.) *Upland Settlement in Britain.* British Archaeological Reports, British Series No. 143, Oxford
RCAHMS 1990. *North-east Perth: an Archaeological Landscape.* HMSO, Edinburgh
Whittle A 1986. *Scord of Brouster.* Oxford University Committee for Archaeology Monograph No. 9

7

THE ENVIRONMENTAL IMPACT OF SHEEP FARMING IN THE SCOTTISH HIGHLANDS

Alexander Mather

Introduction

The coming of commercial sheep farming to the Highlands in the late eighteenth and early nineteenth centuries can be viewed as a small-scale, internal example of what Crosby (1986) terms the 'ecological imperialism' practised by Europeans in new lands overseas. Indeed within a few decades of sheep farming having arrived in the Scottish Highlands, it was also occupying huge areas in Australia and New Zealand. Ironically, we perhaps know rather more of the environmental effects of the arrival of sheep farming in the Antipodes than we do in Scotland.

Myths abound about the nature of the human-environment relationship before and after the arrival of 'ecological imperialism' and of commercial, capitalist farming. In North America, for example, the myth of the 'benign native/devastated colonial' landscape persists (eg. Sale 1990; Denevan 1992). A version of this myth persists also in the Scottish Highlands: for example the Highlands have been described as a 'devastated landscape' (Darling 1947, 1955) which has suffered 'wanton degradation' (Black 1964) and 'exhaustion of its soils and pastures' (Boyd 1967). Sheep and sheep farmers are usually identified as the prime culprits for the alleged degradation. Indeed, according to Darling (1968), 'two centuries of extractive sheep farming... have reduced a rich resource to a state of desolation'.

While there is agreement that the Highland environment was not in a pristine condition when commercial sheep farming was introduced, there is much uncertainty—and perhaps some misconceptions (Smout 1991)—about the nature of the environmental effects to which it gave rise. The aim of this chapter is to identify some of the questions about these effects, rather than to attempt any answers. Two main issues dominate the literature. One concerns the role of sheep farming in relation to woodland clearance, while the other is the much more problematic question of whether sheep farming has caused a deterioration of hill grazings. This chapter concentrates on these two issues, although there are also many other questions about the environmental impacts of sheep farming.

Sheep farming and woodland clearance

A persistent theme has been that the arrival of commercial sheep farming resulted in clearance of woodland in the Highlands. This theme is associated especially with Fraser Darling, but its persistence is reflected in a recent reference in Highland Regional Council's draft indicative forestry strategy, to the effect that woodland was burned to improve grazing for sheep (HRC 1992).

It seems unlikely that the arrival of sheep farming caused a major reduction in the woodland area. This conclusion is reached for two reasons. Firstly, the extent of woodland in mid-eighteenth century Scotland, as depicted on the Roy maps, is almost identical to that reported at the beginning of the twentieth century. In both cases, it was approximately 5 percent (2 and 7 percent respectively in the Lowlands and Highlands) (O'Dell 1953; Acland Committee 1918). The Roy maps need to be viewed with caution (Whittington 1986), and the evidence is not conclusive. It does, however, suggest relative stability in the overall extent of woodland through the period when commercial sheep farming became established. It also confirms that most of the Highlands were already treeless when commercial sheep farming arrived.

Burning

At the more local level, Darling (1949) quotes a specific example of the burning in 1813 of a twelve-mile stretch of 'pine woodland' in Glenstrathfarrar 'to improve the sheep grazing.' The source cited is Stuart and Stuart (1848). This area was already largely treeless in 1755, when Peter May produced a detailed map for the commissioners of Annexed Estates, in whose hands the land lay at the time (Mather 1970). It is difficult to see how a twelve-mile stretch of woodland could have been burned little more than half a century later. The reliability of the alleged example is therefore doubtful.

Together, the Roy and May maps cast serious doubt on whether sheep farming was responsible for a major reduction in the forest area, although burning and grazing may have helped to maintain treelessness. In the longer term, regeneration of some patches of woodland may, of course, have been prevented or impaired. On the other hand, the coming of sheep may have led to some expansion of birch woods in places. It has been suggested that the replacement of cattle by sheep in Strath Glass in the early nineteenth century reduced browsing pressures and allowed birch to expand (Harvie-Brown and Buckley 1895).

What is still unclear is the nature of the effects of sheep farming and associated management practices such as muirburning on non-forest forms of vegetation. In New Zealand, for example, the arrival of sheep farming was marked by the firing of the semi-natural vegetation, in order to remove thorn shrubs and to promote the growth of palatable and nutritious vegetation. To what extent and with what intensity was muirburning carried out in the 'pre-sheep' Highlands, and what changes in the extent and intensity of burning accompanied the arrival of sheep farming?

Sheep farming and the deterioration of hill grazings

In the last quarter of the nineteenth century, reports of deterioration in the quality and productivity of hill grazings began to appear, mainly from the northern Highlands (e.g. MacDonald 1877, 1880; Latham 1883). In most instances the evidence on which the reports were based was anecdotal, and it is possible that some of these reports were simply passed uncritically from source to source. One of the more convincing reports of deterioration, however, came from what was in effect a questionnaire survey of Sutherland sheep farmers. They unanimously reported a deterioration in the 'green land' of their farms (Roberts 1879).

The whole question of possible decline in the carrying capacity of Highland grazings in the late nineteenth century is complicated and confused by the changes then occurring in sheep farming. These changes, stimulated by increased competition from wool and mutton imports from Australia and New Zealand, resulted not only in the clearing of sheep from some areas, but also in changes in emphases away from wedder production. At a time of change in the sheep-farming industry, it may have been tempting to blame environmental causes for the problems facing sheep farmers.

For reasons that are unclear, concern about the possible deterioration of Highland grazings appears to have faded towards the end of the nineteenth century and throughout the first quarter of the twentieth. The Departmental Committee (1922) did, however, find that most witnesses in its inquiry into deer forests thought that their stock-carrying capacity had fallen, and that deterioration had been less in deer forests than on sheep farms. The concern became more prominent again in the 1930s. In 1932 it was claimed that there was 'good evidence to show that the fertility of the Highlands is slowly being drained away' (Orr and Fraser 1932), but unfortunately the detailed evidence was not presented. Nor was it in 1939, when the Department of Agriculture for Scotland concluded that a considerable deterioration had occurred over the previous century (DAS 1939). This perception was shared by the war-time Committee on Hill Sheep Farming in Scotland (Balfour of Burleigh Committee 1944), and one of the objectives of the Hill Farming Act of 1946 was the rehabilitation of hill grazings. The same perception was also shared by several ecologists in the early post-war period, and was epitomised in the 'devastated landscape' hypothesis. By the 1970s, however, it had largely faded.

One interesting question concerns the rise and fall of the perception of deterioration. The rise is not easily explained by objective evidence. It may be speculated that the onset of financial problems as in the 1870s and in the 1930s led to blame being attributed to environmental causes. Hunter (1973) identifies deterioration of pastures as one of the reasons for declining financial performance of sheep farming at this time. It may also be speculated that the publicity afforded to land degradation in the United States, especially in the Dust Bowl and in the Tennessee Valley, may also have been a factor during the 1930s. It is interesting to note echoes of contemporary North American ideas about the relationship between economic and environmental problems in thinking and writing about the Highlands in the period from the 1930s to the 1960s.

A more basic question, however, is simply the evidence for the deterioration of grazings. Such evidence as is quoted usually relates to 'carrying capacities', which often turn out simply to be stock numbers. Stock numbers can, of course, vary for reasons quite unconnected with the state of the environment, especially at times of changing economic circumstances. They are not a reliable indicator of changing carrying capacities or of general ecological health. Unfortunately, few other measures are available.

Lambing performance is one alternative indicator of the relationship between sheep and their environment, partly depending as it does on the nutritional level of the ewes. This performance can be estimated, in general if not in precise terms, from the annual agricultural census carried out in early June, and available in summary form for individual parishes. An indication of lambing performance can be obtained simply by relating ewe numbers to numbers of sheep of less than one year of age. This has been done for the mainland parishes of Inverness-shire and Ross-shire, for a period from 1890 to 1975 (Mather 1978).

This approach is not without its limitations. Lambing percentages can vary for reasons quite unconnected with the possible deterioration of hill grazings. The intensity of management, extent of improved land, and possible declines in the quality of breeding stock (in a system where breeding replacements are retained) could all have an influence. The agricultural census also has its limitations, and the effort of extracting data for a sizeable number of parishes over a period of around 100 years is time-consuming and tedious. Furthermore, the parish is an unsatisfactory unit of analysis, containing as it does mixtures of farm sizes and land types. Changes in the area grazed and the implementation of land-settlement programmes are also complications. It is clear, therefore, that the results of lambing-percentage analyses need to be viewed with caution.

Nevertheless, these results are interesting. A clear spatial pattern emerges. The eastern parishes clearly display rising trends, but the picture is very different in the west (Fig. 7.1). In west-coast parishes such as Glenelg, clear downward trends are apparent, in some cases at an annual rate averaging one percentage point every four years (Fig. 7.2). It is noticeable that neighbouring parishes show similar trends, and that occasional reference to performances on individual west-coast hill-sheep farms also indicate decline. For example, Stewart (1967) reports that the lambing percentages on one farm near Oban fell from 78 in 1890 to 62 in 1966, and on another from 86 to 71 over the same period.

Again it must be emphasised that declining trends in lambing percentages do not necessarily indicate deterioration of hill grazings. On the other hand, downturns in the productivity of any form of agriculture over the last hundred years are very unusual, and the results of the analyses suggest that a closer look is merited.

If the provisional conclusion is that some circumstantial evidence exists that may point to a possible deterioration in hill grazings, the question then

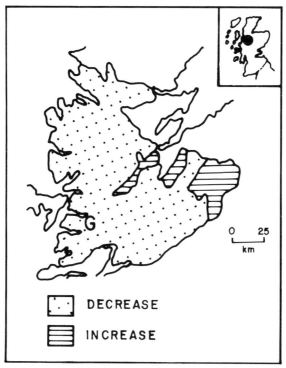

Fig 7.1: Generalised trends in apparent lambing percentages, upland parishes of
mainland Inverness-shire and Ross-shire, 1890-1975
G = Glenelg Parish (source: modified after Mather 1978)

arises as to the cause of this decline. Even if it is assumed that the cause is
environmental (rather than genetic or related to management), much
uncertainty exists. Soil erosion and other forms of deterioration of soils,
changes in vegetation, and even factors such as changing climatic conditions
could all be hypothesised as causes.

The depletion of soil nutrients as a result of burning and of cropping of
wool and mutton over a long period was assumed by some commentators to
be the cause of deterioration. This assumption, however, has been questioned
in the light of work carried out more recently. Several attempts have been
made to compile nutrient balance sheets for hill land: one example is the
work of Crisp (1966). The general conclusion has been that nutrient gains
from precipitation exceed losses through burning and animal production.
Phosphorus, of which there appears to be continuing depletion, is an
important exception (Sydes and Miller 1988). Most of this work has been
carried out in eastern Scotland, and other nutrients may be in deficit in
western Scotland where fires may be larger, hotter and more frequent (Hobbs
and Gimingham 1987). It remains to be established whether the apparent
decline in lambing performance in parts of western Scotland is in any way
related to nutrient trends.

The significance of precipitation inputs in areas of steep slopes and much direct run off may be questioned, but the question of possible re-distribution of nutrients is perhaps more pertinent. Much of the grazing effort of hill sheep in the Highlands is concentrated on the small areas of 'green-land', many of which occupy areas of former cultivation. But much of the non-grazing time of the sheep is spent in other areas, perhaps on higher ground. Nutrients absorbed during grazing on the greens may therefore be returned in the form of dung and urine to the 'black-land' areas of lower grazing value. It is possible, therefore, that there may be a re-distribution of nutrients away from the key grazing areas, even if no overall nutrient depletion takes place. This hypothesis accords with the results of Roberts' (1879) survey, in which Sutherland sheep farmers reported deterioration of the 'green-land' but not of the 'black-land'.

It is, however, no more than a hypothesis, and the deterioration of the 'green-land' reported by Roberts could have resulted from other causes. For example a reduction in grazing intensities, at a time of a downturn in the fortunes of sheep farming in the 1870s and the removal of wedder stocks, could have given rise to the 'increased fogginess' of the vegetation on some of the greens, as reported by the Sutherland farmers. In other words, a lessening of sheep-farming pressures could have brought about the apparent change in vegetation.

There is also the question of the inter-relationship between sheep and deer grazing, and of presumably increasing numbers of deer as deer forests expanded towards the end of the century. Long-term trends in deer and sheep numbers alike are difficult to establish, but an inverse relationship between changes in deer and sheep densities for the recent period is reported by Clutton-Brock and Albon (1992). Last century, one of the witnesses to the

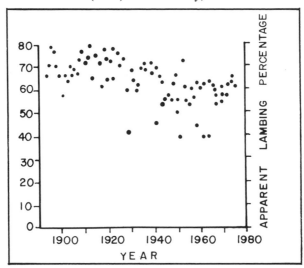

Fig 7.2: Apparent lambing percentages, parish of Glenelg, 1890-1975
(source: compiled from data in the parish summaries of the Agricultural Census)

Crofters Commission, a sheep farmer from Arnisdale in Glenelg, considered that any deterioration that had occurred had resulted from deer rather than sheep (Crofters Commission 1884). A further question is that of soil erosion, and the possible resultant loss of soil nutrients and vegetation. Tivy (1957) drew attention to sheep-induced erosion in the Southern Uplands, but little detailed work has been reported from the Highlands. There is, however, some evidence of increased erosional activity in recent centuries. Innes (1983a, 1983b) found evidence of an increased occurrence of mass movements over the last three centuries, possibly resulting from increased burning. Ballantyne (1991) and Ballantyne and Whittington (1987) have identified grazing as a possible but unconfirmed cause of accelerated erosion. In short the cause(s) of increases in erosion rates have not as yet been established, nor have any practical effects on sheep farming (in terms of loss of nutrients and herbage) been identified.

Other environmental effects

This chapter has focused on two alleged environmental effects of sheep farming that have given rise to controversy—the immediate impact on the woodland area, and the longer term influence on land productivity. There are various other possible environmental effects, of both direct and indirect types.

Local grazing effects on vegetation in parts of the Highlands are reported by Thompson et al. (1987). For example tufted hair grass (*Deschampsia caespitosa*) in corries and steep slopes may be derived from over-grazed tall-herb or fern-dominated communities, and high-altitude moss heath may give way to grass heath. Both of these cases may involve grazing by deer as well as by sheep.

Another possible effect is an increase in numbers of carrion-eating birds following the arrival of commercial sheep farming and, presumably, increasing numbers of carcasses of sheep and lambs. On the other hand, predatory birds may have come under pressure of persecution, especially on grouse moors and in other areas intensively managed for sport. Perhaps this is a reminder that marked spatial variations may have existed within the Highlands, and that sweeping generalisations are perhaps unwise.

In the long term, the upheavals in human settlement patterns and changes in population densities that accompanied the arrival of sheep farming may have had a profound if indirect effect. Some inland straths and glens were emptied of their human populations, and local labour intensity on the land probably declined sharply in the cleared areas. These changes may have paved the way for the eventual growth in deer populations in the emptied areas. At the same time, new human pressures were brought to bear in the new crofting townships and other resettlement areas along the coast.

Conclusion

The impact of sheep farming on the Highland environment is uncertain. One possible aspect of this impact—that leading to deterioration of grazing quality—has attracted attention for more than a hundred years but is still unresolved. Indeed, we seem to have progressed little from the position reached by the Crofters Commission more than a hundred years ago: 'The question whether there is progressive deterioration of the natural mountain pasture of the Highlands is one which opens a wide field of discussion and on which a conflict of opinion exists' (Crofters Commission, 1884). At various times over the last hundred years the physical sustainability of sheep farming has been questioned, but the issue has never been satisfactorily resolved. Various reasons may combine to explain this continuing uncertainty. Technical problems confront any attempts to address the question. Institutional issues are probably also involved: government structures and machinery for ensuring sustainability have been lacking over most of the period.

Several specific issues deserve closer scrutiny and further work. One is the role and nature of burning, and indeed also of other land-management practices, in pre- and post-sheep times. The potential for 'before and after' studies is of course limited by the availability of documentary records such as maps, rentals, and game books, and long series of such records, spanning the arrival of sheep farming, rarely exist. Perhaps the best that can be realistically hoped for is that better, clearer and fuller general pictures or models of pre- and post-sheep land management can be constructed. Another issue is the possible role of individual estate and sheep-farm records in providing measures of performance (in terms of lambing percentages, for example). It would also be informative to widen the area of analyses of lambing performance at the parish level, by including the islands and Argyll and Sutherland, as well as mainland Inverness-shire and Ross-shire. It would certainly be useful to subject these parish data to further statistical analyses.

The arrival of commercial sheep farming in the Highlands was accompanied by a new regime of land management, and a radical change in population distribution and in the pattern of settlement. Both direct and indirect environmental effects are likely to have resulted: there is little doubt that the Highland environment has been significantly modified by sheep farming over the last two hundred years. There is much more doubt about the nature, pattern and magnitude of that modification. The social impact of commercial sheep farming in the Highlands has attracted a tremendous amount of attention. As yet the environmental impact is much less well understood, although its effects may be both wide-ranging and variable from locality to locality. In many other parts of the world, similar social upheavals have been accompanied by apparent environmental disruption. It remains to be established whether the environmental consequences in the Highlands were as great as the social ones.

Bibliography

Acland Committee 1918. *Final Report of the Forestry Sub-Committee of the Reconstruction Committee*, Cd. 8881. HMSO, London

Balfour of Burleigh Committee. 1944. *Report of the Committee on Hill Sheep Farming in Scotland.* Cmd. 6494. HMSO, London

Ballantyne C K 1991. Holocene geomorphic activity in the Scottish Highlands. *Scottish Geographical Magazine* 107: 84-98

Ballantyne C K, Whittington G W 1987. Niveo-aeolian sand deposits on An Teallach, Wester Ross, Scotland. *Trans. Royal Society of Edinburgh: Earth Sciences* 78: 51-63

Black J N 1964. The ecology of land use in Scotland. *Trans.Botanical Society of Edinburgh* 40: 1-12

Boyd J M 1967. Land-use planning for wildlife and natural resources in the north-west Highlands. In: Duffey E (ed) *The Biotic Effects of Public Pressures on the environment.* NERC, Monks Wood

Clutton-Brock T H, Albon S D 1992. Trial and error in the Highlands. *Nature* 358: 11-12

Crisp D T 1966. Input and output of minerals for an area of Pennine moorland: the importance of precipitation, drainage, peat erosion and animals. *Journal of Applied Ecology* 3:327-48

Crofters Commission 1884. *Report of HM Commissioners of Inquiry into the Condition of Crofters and Cottars in the Highlands and Islands of Scotland.* C.3980. HMSO, London

Crosby A W 1986. *Ecological Imperialism.* Cambridge University Press, Cambridge

Darling F Fraser 1947. *Natural History in the Highlands and Islands.* Collins, London

Darling F Fraser 1949. History of the Scottish forests. *Scottish Geographical Magazine* 65: 137-37

Darling F Fraser 1955. *West Highland Survey.* Oxford University Press, Oxford

Darling F Fraser 1968. The ecology of land use in the Highlands and Islands. In: Thomson D S, Grimble I (eds) *The Future of the Highlands.* RKP, London

Department of Agriculture for Scotland 1939. The stock-carrying capacity of hill grazings in Scotland. *DAS Miscellaneous Publications* 15. HMSO, Edinburgh

Denevan W M 1992. The pristine myth: the landscape of the Americas in 1492. *Annals, Association of American Geographers* 82: 369-85

Departmental Committee 1922. *Report of the Departmental Committee Appointed in 1919 to Enquire and Report with Regard to Lands in Scotland used as Deer Forests.* Cmd. 1636, HMSO, London.

Harvie-Brown J A, Buckley T E 1895. *A Vertebrate Fauna of the Moray Basin.* Douglas, Edinburgh

Highland Regional Council 1992. *Draft Highland Region Indicative Forestry Strategy and Survey Report.* HRC, Inverness

Hobbs R J, Gimingham C H 1987. Vegetation, fire and herbivore interactions in heathland. *Advances in Ecological Research* 16: 87-173

Hunter J 1973. Sheep and deer: Highland sheep farming 1850-1900. *Northern Scotland* 1:199-222

Innes J L 1983a. Lichenometric dating of debris flow deposits in the Scottish Highlands. *Earth Surface Processes and Landforms* 8: 579-88

Innes J L 1983b. Land use changes in the Scottish Highlands in the 19th century: the role of pasture degeneration. *Scottish Geographical Magazine* 99: 141-9

Latham R 1883. The deterioration of mountain pastures and suggestions for their improvement. *Trans. Highland and Agricultural Society of Scotland (THASS).* 4th series. 15: 111-30

MacDonald J 1877. On the agriculture of the county of Ross and Cromarty. *THASS.* 4th series. 9: 67-209

MacDonald J 1880. On the agriculture of the county of Sutherland. *THASS.* 4th series.

12: 1-89

Mather A S 1970. Pre-1745 land use and conservation in a Highland glen. *Scottish Geographical Magazine* 86: 159-70

Mather A S 1978. The alleged deterioration in hill grazings in the Scottish Highlands. *Biological Conservation* 14: 181-95

O'Dell A C 1953. A view of Scotland in the middle of the eighteenth century. *Scottish Geographical Magazine* 102: 18-28

Orr J B, Fraser A H H 1932. Restoring the fertility of Scottish sheep grazings. *THASS*. 5th series. 44: 64-85

Roberts C G 1879. Sutherland reclamations. *Journal of the Royal Agricultural Society of England*. 2nd series. 15: 397-487

Sale K 1990. *The Conquest of Paradise: Christopher Columbus and the Columbian Legacy*. A P Knopf, New York

Smout T C 1991. Highland land use before 1800: misconceptions, evidence and realities. In: Bachell A (ed.) *Highland Land Use: Four Historical and Conservation Perspectives*. NCCS, Inverness

Stewart I M 1967. Sheep capacity of the poorer Highland hills. *Scottish Agriculture* 46: 135-38

Stuart J S, Stuart C E 1848. *Lays of the deer forest*. Vol. II. Edinburgh and London

Sydes C, Miller G R 1988. Range management and nature conservation in the British uplands. In: Usher M B, Thompson D B A (eds). *Ecological Change in the Uplands*. Blackwell, Oxford

Thompson D B A, Galbraith H, Horsfield D 1987. Ecology and resources of Britain's mountain plateaux: land use conflicts and impacts. In: Bell M, Bunce R G H (eds.). *Agriculture and Conservation in the Hills and Uplands*. Institute of Terrestrial Ecology, Grange-over-Sands

Tivy J 1957. Influence des facteurs biologiques sur l'érosion dans les Southern Uplands écossais. *Revue Géomorphique Dynamique* 8: 9-19

Whittington G W 1986. The Roy map: protracted and fair copies. *Scottish Geographical Magazine* 102: 18-28; 66-73.

8

CHANGING DEER NUMBERS IN THE SCOTTISH HIGHLANDS SINCE 1780

John S Smith

Introduction

The Scottish Highlands are the upland environments north of the Central Lowlands, including the Hebrides. The land area is about 30,000kms and the present red deer population living in open habitats there runs to about 270,000 (Red Deer Commission Annual Report 1991). Red deer evolved as a low ground woodland-heathland species (Clutton-Brock and Albon 1989). As the natural woodland shrank in extent, increasingly open habitats retained the title 'forest', while the identical title was applied to those treeless environments subsequently occupied by deer as their low ground territories were developed for agricultural purposes. Although the term 'deer forest' may seem to imply land populated only by deer, without other large grazing animals, even in the nineteenth century, and certainly in the present century, there were few deer forests without at least one additional grazing competitor on at least part of their ground. Whitehead (1960) noted that it is very difficult to distinguish between deer forests grazed by sheep and lightly stocked sheep-farms where deer are stalked and shot. He therefore suggested the best definition of a deer forest was deer stalking terrain. This chapter concentrates on assembling historical clues pertinent to reconstructing changes in extent and number of red deer in the Highlands since the late eighteenth century.

Trends in deer numbers to 1780

By the end of the medieval period, most of the low-lying areas within the Scottish Highlands had been cleared of their natural woodland for agriculture, fuel or grazing ground. By the seventeenth century, native woodlands survived only in the remoter areas. Despite the probable contraction of red deer range to these areas, travellers such as Pennant occasionally commented on successful pinewood regeneration, as at the Ballochbuie on Deeside. This might suggest that the prevailing deer numbers here were relatively low. On the other hand deer numbers remained sufficiently high to permit the classic deer drives in Atholl and Mar, but it

County	Parish	Old Statistical Account	New Statistical Account
Aberdeenshire	Kennay	O	
	Tullynestle		O
	Lumphanan		◆
	Glen Muick	◆	
	Auchindoir		*
	Crathie - Braemar	*	O
	Alford	◆	◆
	Birse	◆	◆
	Strathdon		
Argyllshire	Callandar		◆
	Kildalton		◆
	Duncon		◆
	Jura	O	◆
	Ardchattan		O
	Kilfinichen	◆	*
	Kilmelfort		◆
	Glen Orchy		◆
	Morvern	O	
	Lismore Appin	◆	
	Torosay	◆	
	Kilmalie		◆
Invernessshire	Portree		◆
	Kilmorack		◆
	Laggan	◆	◆
	North Uist		◆
	Harris		◆
	Moy & Dalarossie		◆
	Kilmalie	O	◆
	Kingussie	◆	
	Boleskine Abertarff		*
	Glen Urquhart Moriston	◆	*
	Strath (Skye)	◆	*
	Portree	◆	*
	Glen Elg		
	Alvie		
	South Uist		
	Small Isles		
	Lochgoilhead/Inch		
Angus	Edzell	O	
	Tannadice	◆	◆
	Loch Lee	O	
Elginshire	Ardlach		◆

County	Parish	Old Statistical Account	New Statistical Account
Perthshire	Auchterarder	O	◆
	Auchtergaven	O	◆
	Kenmore		◆
	Fortingall		*
	Blair Atholl		*
	Comrie	◆	O
	Moulin	◆	
	Longforgan	◆	
	Dowally		*
	Doune		
	Killin	◆	
Ross and Cromarty	Kincardine		O
	Kiltearn		◆
	Rosskeen		◆
	Fodderty		◆
	Applecross		◆
	Barvas		◆
	Lochs	◆	O
	Kintail	◆	◆
	Dingwall	*	
	Glen Shiel		
	Lochalsh		O
	Contin		◆
	Kilmuir Easter		*
Sutherlandshire	Loth		*
	Kildonan		◆
	Edderachillis		O
	Durness	◆	O
	Farr		O
	Rogart	◆	*
	Golspie	*	O
	Dornoch		O
Banffshire	Kirkmichael	◆	*
	Inveravon		O
	Boharm		O
	Mortlach		
Caithness	Latheron	*	◆
	Wick		◆
	Reay		◆
Nairnshire	Radford		◆
	Rothiemurchus		◆

Fig 8.1: References to Red Deer in Old and New Statistical Accounts—;   O mention/occasional visit   ◆ present   ★ deer forests

may be argued that the very considerable manpower resources and time devoted to this exercise might reflect the relatively low densities on the ground, as much as the limited technology for killing. There is thus some support for the argument expressed by Hart-Davis (1978) and accepted without comment by Clutton-Brock and Albon (1989) that 'throughout most of the country, numbers (of red deer) were probably declining during the seventeenth and eighteenth centuries'.

Colonel Thomas Thornton during an 1804 Kingussie-based sporting tour made daily expeditions into the hills, reporting ample grouse and ptarmigan, but only came across red deer very occasionally. Other sportsmen, for example Charles St John, appear to have had similar experiences. St John spent six October days within Sutherland in the 1840s with scarcely any deer sighted. William Scrope (1838) noted:

> The number of deer that wander over the vast forests of Sutherland cannot well be ascertained. About thirty years ago, an opinion prevailed that it amounted to 3000. The introduction of sheep farms and other causes, have materially lessened that number, if indeed it was a correct one. So that the harts, hinds and calves, of all ages, taken collectively, do not probably at present, exceed the number of 1500.

Several authors record increasing concern by the few landowners who sought to maintain traditional deer forests in the core areas of Atholl, Blackmount, Glenartney, Glen Fiddich, Invercauld and Mar in the face of the deleterious effects of deer poaching by nearby resident populations. The context implies poaching within the forest rather than the taking of marauding deer. Adam Watson's analysis (1983) of the Duke of Fife's diary over the period 1783-1792 reveals this concern over scarcity of deer. The severe actions taken by this landowner against poaching led to significant improvements of shooting success rates on Mar ground. Pine regeneration was also recorded in the diary on sites where it has not occurred since. In the second half of the eighteenth century, the human populations of those areas still ranged by deer grew considerably, in some cases doubling between 1755 and 1792. On the better grassy uplands of the Central and Western Highlands, and in parts of Sutherland, estates had already been cleared for sheep-ranching, with the likely result hinted at by Scrope, that deer and sheep were in competition for grazing space. James Robertson (1813) notes 'that although there be no regular forest in all of the county (Invernessshire), except that of Lochiel alone, yet there are straggling deer to be met within almost every part of the mountainous districts'. In the single mention of fence damage, sheep are identified as the offenders.

While the analysis of estate diaries pioneered by Watson offers useful detailed information on one deer forest, the only potential comprehensive cover for the Scottish Highlands remains the *Old* and *New Statistical Accounts*. A parish by parish search in the 'deer forest counties' has been attempted, the results of which are summarised in Fig 8.1. A selection from the *Old Statistical Account* follows which serves to convey a flavour of the evidence for deer presence right at the end of the eighteenth century.

The Earl of Fife and Mr Farquharson of Invercauld 'have each of them, extensive forest which are well-stocked with red and roe deer. From the great care and attention which has been paid to these animals for some years past, they are now numerous and domesticated...'(*Crathie and Braemar*)

'In the forest of Glen Fiddich, there is an abundance of red deer—a thousand or more with a few roes. The farmers round it think them by far too numerous...'(*Mortlach*)

'His Grace (the Duke of Atholl) has a tract of 100,000 acres reserved chiefly for them, and it is computed that not less than 4000 feed there regularly...' (*Blair Atholl*)

'The deer of the forest are very troublesome to the people of the glen in summer and winter, by eating their corn...' (*Lorn*)

Other parish entries document the arrival of a quadruped competitor:

'Ben More, formerly a deer forest, is now converted into a sheep walk' (*Killin*)

'Sheep will soon banish them (the red deer), as they cannot endure to pasture with them' (*Appin*)

'The mountains now being flocked with sheep, may in the course of a few years, banish them from the Isle of Mull' (*Kilfinichen*)

The incompatibility of deer and sheep hinted at in Mull and Appin was echoed by Darling (1955). He suggested that the removal of forest and the much more restricted secondary growth areas, along with heavy exploitation of the ground by sheep, would inevitably cause reduction in deer numbers.

Trends in deer numbers during the nineteenth century

The publication of Scrope's *Days of Deerstalking* (1838) provides some data on the period between the *Old* and *New Statistical Accounts*. In some cases, land cleared of deer for sheep was returned to deer forest as the sporting vogue developed (Hunter 1973). Scrope's book suggests that deer populations could build up rapidly under these circumstances. He notes that the Glen Tilt deer population numbered only 100 in 1776. In the period between 1786 and 1796, sheep were removed from the glen. By the date the book was published, numbers were computed at about 7,000, although Scrope suggests the correct figure was between 5,000 and 6,000—on the basis of a count carried out by himself during two completed deer drives which took place on the same day. The hunting of red deer was almost exclusively confined to the harts. As he expressed it 'hinds are, of course, far more numerous than the harts, as none but yeld hinds are killed except by accident'. During one stalk, 'there were slain three hinds, that nobody would own to, and an exceedingly promising young fawn, repudiated by all'. Scrope cites an account of Coul deer forest written by Sir George Stuart Mackenzie, who notes a remarkable increase in red and roe deer over a twenty year period.

As Sir George expresses it:

> It was supposed that the introduction of sheep had driven them away; but although
> this may have been one great cause, it was neither the sheep nor the shepherds or
> their dogs, that occasioned the extreme scarcity, but the great extent to which
> poaching was carried out...every Highlander having formerly been in possession of
> a gun of some sort.

The accounts of rapid growth in deer numbers registered around this time appear to have resulted from a relatively high hind population, the ease of movement (in the absence of barriers) for herds to occupy alternative ground, and reduced poaching activities, as deer forests became keepered and managed as potential sources of income. The winter feeding of deer with corn and hay is recorded at Glenartney (Scrope 1838).

Despite the concern registered over grazing competition between sheep and deer in the early nineteenth century, there appears to have been no modern fieldwork systematically studying this problem. Clutton-Brock and Albon (1989) suggest that the presence of sheep is associated with reduced use by deer of the fescue swards preferred by both species. At Glenartney, Scrope records that part of the ground carried cattle all the year round, but the sheep were removed 'as they were found to feed upon the best deer pasture and because the shepherds disturbed the stags with their dogs'. By the 1840s, around 30 'new' forests had been established (Hunter 1973), mostly from ground cleared of sheep by landowners keen to explore the commercial possibilities of sporting revenues, despite rents being low by comparison with those obtained from sheep tenants.

Once again, entries in the *New Statistical Account* reveal considerable differences across the Highlands:

> 'Red deer are not so plentiful as they were fifty years ago, yet there is still
> a good number of them. As an end has been put to deer stalking, and as all
> the proprietors have shown a desire of late to prevent their extermination,
> they are at present rapidly on the increase...' (*Torosay, Argyllshire*)

> 'The immense forest of Glen Avon is now being stocked with deer...the
> duke of Richmond's portions letting at £3,000pa...' (*Kirkmichael*)

> 'Before the introduction of sheep farming, deer were to be found in
> considerable numbers on the estates of Langwell, Braemore and Dunbeath,
> but for many years back, are rarely to be met with' (*Latheron*)

> 'Hare and roe seldom seen, and deer are not nearly so numerous as many
> of the older inhabitants remember them to have been...the grazing on
> which the deer in former times pastured, is now stocked with sheep, and
> being continually annoyed by shepherd's dogs' (*Kintail*)

> 'Deer stalking has, of late, been revived with great ardour in the
> district...and in the few other remote parts of the Highlands where the stag
> is now to be met with' (*Kildonan*)

These entries confirm the perceived incompatibility of sheep and deer on the same ground, and also imply considerable differences in deer density even in their traditional upland ground. McConnochie (1923) notes that while Mar in 1826 was advertised as 'filled to profusion with red deer of which there are supposed to be at least 3,000', Strathconan when advertised in 1836 included no reference to deer. The advertisements sometimes reveal a flexibility of possibilities to encourage prospective tenants. In 1812, Glen Feshie was advertised as 'adapted as either a summer grazing for black cattle or for shooting grounds to a sportsman who might wish to preserve the tract for deer, moor-game and ptarmigan, all of which abound in the surrounding hills, and with which it would be abundantly stocked in a very short time if carefully kept for that purpose' (McConnochie 1923).

The speed of sporting development, however, remained slow until the inaccessibility of the Highlands to southerners was reduced by the extension of the railway net in the second half of the nineteenth century. New forests were developed. Hart-Davis's analyses (1978) of the Glen Feshie gamebooks from the 1830s onwards reveals initially high grouse bags, but hardly any deer. On newly created forests, the main pursuit (and in some cases, the main attraction) were the moorgame, but over decades, deer colonised such areas and quickly increased in number. This growth in deer population was favoured by lack of interest in culling hinds, and possibly increased 'vermin' control, although the latter would most benefit grouse numbers. Indeed, in the 1860s, the Balmoral factor reported that two highly successful grouse breeding years had made them so numerous that they greatly impeded successful stalking.

The second half of the nineteenth century witnessed increasing attempts to manage deer forests. By the 1850s the popularity of stalking meant that forests available for rent were quickly taken up by tenants (Hunter 1973). The peaking of wool prices in the middle 1860s, combined with pasture deterioration, meant that deer forests developed their own commercial momentum. New forests were created, especially in the Northern Highlands, while existing forests expanded outwards and often altitudinally downwards into ground under agricultural uses. By the 1880s the Napier Commission judged that hill land was worth 50 percent more under deer than sheep, and this profit margin of deer forest rentals relative to sheep farms continued to grow.

The process of deer forest creation has been little researched in terms of deer populations, although much has been written on the economic impact. The game book at Ardtornish, Morvern, begins in 1853. Grouse were shot but deer were at first seldom sighted. The spread of heather and its better performance favoured increases in grouse bags, while the red deer spread in naturally. The sporting potential was improved through better keepering, and game-money was paid to keepers on stags and grouse shot. Keepers were also paid vermin bounties. The Langwell gamebook reveals a similar process (Hart-Davis 1978).

Little is known about management policies on culling rates, although in the early days of Coulin Forest, the keeper estimated that around 400 deer were on the ground, and recommended that around 10 percent of the stags could be shot each year 'if the place is kept properly'. By 1890 there were 130 deer forests extending to around 2,500,000 acres. Deer were becoming detrimental to the crofting population through marauding, while the Highland Land League viewed parts of deer forests as areas of potential land settlement. Both the Napier Commission and the 1895 Deer Forest Commission recommended a curb on deer forest expansion, but neither were successful, as by 1910 the acreage had risen to 3,500,000 acres.

Trends of deer numbers in the twentieth century

Some estimates for stag and hind cull are provided by Grimble (1901), although the data is not completely comprehensive. The hind cull survey of 1883 indicates that 'most of the large forests kill more than 100 hinds each season'. Grimble calculated a total hind cull of around 5,300 per annum. From the 86 deer forests for which data was available to him, a total of 4,600 stags were shot on average per annum. The text contains further indications of the speed with which deer colonised freshly cleared ground, together with an appreciation of the benefits of woodland wintering ground and of 'proper treatment and care for the deer'.

A rather more comprehensive survey carried out just before the Second World War (Whitehead 1960) and based on a questionnaire suggests an annual cull of 10,000 stags and 8,000 hinds (Clutton-Brock and Albon 1989). Whitehead quotes the deer forest Departmental Committee Report (1922) for a statement that at least 25 head of red deer must on average be available for each stag killed. However there is no authoritative discussion of the validity of this ratio, or how it might change with management practices. However, if correct, it would imply a red deer population of around 250,000 before the Second World War, and about half that number in Grimble's day. Clutton-Brock argues that deer numbers declined substantially during the Second World War as a result of increased shooting for meat and poaching activities.

In the post-war period, there was growing concern over marauding on agricultural ground and public disquiet over widespread organised poaching. In the period between 1953 and 1960, counts carried out by the Nature Conservancy via Fraser Darling resulted in an estimated population of 155,000. Following the establishment of the Red Deer Commission as a result of the Deer (Scotland) Act of 1959, organised counts over much of the ground gave an estimate of 185,000 red deer (Clutton-Brock and Albon 1989). The increase in numbers since then has taken place despite encroachment of forestry onto deer ground, and at a time when there is increasing concern over deer impact on woodland, grazing and soils.

Conclusion

It is difficult to comment on the possible environmental impacts of red deer in the Scottish Highlands in the absence of reliable historical data on population numbers and distribution. The social and economic impacts have been researched in recent decades, but the environmental impact scarcely at all, despite the admirable lead given by Fraser Darling in his *West Highland Survey*. Red deer densities vary very considerably in the Highlands of Scotland at the present time, and the historical data assembled in this chapter demonstrate that this pattern of variance has been repeated in space and time over the last two hundred years. There seems, however, to be little doubt that in the later twentieth century numbers are very much larger than they were at the beginning of the nineteenth.

Hill sheep and red deer frequently share the same ground, and isolating their individual impacts under these circumstances must be difficult. Geomorphological investigations in the Scottish Highlands have identified evidence for increased rates of soil erosion over the last few hundred years (Ballantyne 1991). However it has proved impossible to separate changes in grazing pressures from climatic fluctuations or indeed muirburn management procedures as possible causes. It seems that one of the most pertinent problems facing upland land managers in the future will be to distinguish natural erosion from other forms of damage, and take appropriate action. The historical data suggests very considerable swings in population numbers of deer, superimposed on sheep numbers, all related to management decisions. Deer have proved very adaptable in spreading from core areas to colonise new ground. In addition, weather-driven population fluctuations in animal mortality is another variable to be borne in mind. Only the impact of growing red deer numbers on native woodlands seems to be firmly established.

Future research might proceed along the lines of combining biological studies of red deer with companion studies of contemporary geomorphological processes on the same ground, and better still, though doubtless difficult, similar studies on ground grazed by both sheep and deer. The study of estate game books would enhance our knowledge of the wildlife composition of sporting estates over the last 140 years.

It would therefore be wise to err on the side of caution before making definitive statements on the impact of deer on the environment, although it is perhaps fitting to remember that Fraser Darling did suggest an optimum population of 60,000 red deer in the Highland Counties.

Bibliography

Ballantyne C K. 1991. Holocene geomorphic activity in the Scottish Highlands. *Scottish Geographical Magazine* 107: 84-98

Clutton-Brock T H, Albon S D. 1989. *Red Deer in the Highlands*. Oxford

Darling F F. 1955. *West Highland Survey*. Oxford

Deer Forest Commission   1895. *Royal Commission on the Highlands and Islands Appointed to Inquire into Land Occupied for the Purpose of Deer Forest or Other Sporting Purposes or for Grazing.*

Deer Forest Departmental Committee. 1922. *Report of the Departmental Committee Appointed in 1919 to Enquire and Report with Regard to Lands in Scotland Used as Deer Forests*. Cmd.1636. HMSO, London.

Grimble A. 1901. *Deerstalking and the Deer Forests of Scotland*. London

Hart-Davis D. 1978. *Monarchs of the Glen*. London

Hunter J. 1973. Sheep and deer: Highland sheep farming 1850-1900. *Northern Scotland* (1) : 199-222

McConnochie A I. 1923. *The Deer and Deer Forests of Scotland: Historical, Descriptive, Sporting.* London

Napier Commission 1884 *Commission of Inquiry into the Condition of Crofters and Cottars of the Highlands and Islands of Scotland.* 4 vols. Q 42269

New Statistical Account of Scotland

Old Statistical Account of Scotland

Red Deer Commission. 1991. *Annual Report*

Robertson J. 1813. *General View of the Agriculture of the County of Inverness.* Edinburgh

Scrope W. 1838. *Days of Deerstalking.* London

Watson A. 1983. Eighteenth century deer numbers and pine regeneration near Braemar, Scotland. *Biological Conservation* (25): 289-305

Whitehead G K. 1960. *The Deer Stalking Grounds of Great Britain and Ireland.* London

9

SCOTTISH SALMON
The Relevance of Studies of Historical Catch Data

David W Summers

Introduction

The Scottish commercial fishery for Atlantic salmon (*Salmo salar* L.) has a long history. The traditional method of catching salmon was by net and coble fishing in rivers and estuaries, although in some rivers, traps known as 'cruives' were also used. From about the 1820s, new fisheries appeared along the coast and these used 'stake' and 'bag' nets which trapped salmon as they migrated towards their native rivers. These new methods of fishing rapidly spread during the nineteenth century, and by the end of that century commercial salmon fishing in Scotland largely took place in the sea. There have been no fundamental changes in the methods used in Scotland to catch salmon both at sea and in rivers for over 150 years. In recent times most remaining net and coble fisheries and many sea fisheries have closed, largely as a result of commercial failure, or buyouts by angling interests (Williamson 1991).

Detailed records of the catches obtained at several fisheries still exist for up to 200 years. These records are largely from old established companies rather than from leased fisheries, but more fragmentary data can be found for some smaller concerns. However, there are many potential problems in using such data to describe long-term changes in salmon populations. Catches may vary as a result of factors like the weather, freshwater discharge and changes in fishing effort (Shearer 1986). In order to speculate on long-term changes in a salmon population from catch data a thorough knowledge of a fishery's history is required. The collection and interpretation of long-term salmon catch data is therefore largely a historical problem.

During the recent past there has been an increase in interest in historical salmon catch data, both in Europe and North America (Bielak and Power 1988; de Groot 1991; Gee and Milner 1980; George 1982; Martin and Mitchell 1985; Menzies and Smart 1966; Mills 1987; Shearer 1985, 1986, 1988, 1989, 1992; Summers 1989, 1992; Taylor 1986; Thibault 1991). This chapter considers the extent to which investigations into historical salmon catch data have relevance in terms of an understanding of the population dynamics of Scottish salmon.

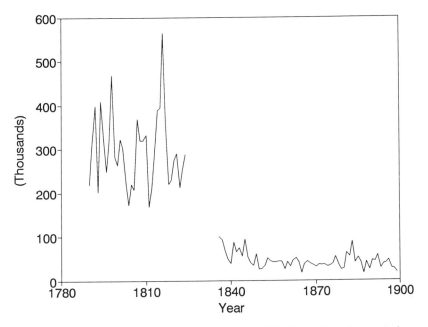

Fig. 9.1: Total weight (lbs) of grilse and salmon combined caught each year at the Raik, Midchingle, and Pot & Fords net and coble fisheries, River Dee, Aberdeen, 1790-1824 and 1836-1899. Data: Anon (1825); Aberdeen Salmon Company records; Aberdeen Harbour Board records

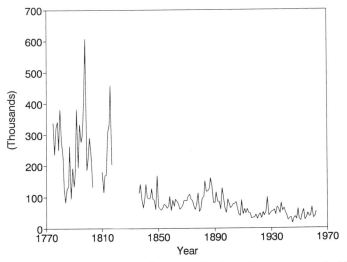

Fig. 9.2: Weight (lbs) of grilse and salmon combined caught each year at the Nether Don Fishery, Aberdeen, 1775-1803, 1810-1817, and 1836-1962. Data: Burnett (1951); Anon (1825, 1836); Aberdeen Salmon Company (unpubl.)

Long-term changes in Scottish salmon catches

Catch data normally take the form of numbers of grilse (i.e. those fish, which after entering the sea as smolts, only spend one winter there before returning to freshwater to spawn) and salmon (fish which spend two or more winters at sea before returning to spawn), although fishermen do not always distinguish between grilse and salmon with absolute accuracy (Shearer 1986). Where data are available in this form, it is presented as the total catch from a given smolt year (which is the number of grilse caught in the following year plus the number of salmon caught in the year after that). All salmon are assumed to have returned after two winters in the sea, which the majority do (Martin and Mitchell 1985).

Figures 9.1-9.5 show long series of catch data from net fisheries in the rivers Dee, Don, Spey and Tweed, and sea nets in Aberdeen Bay. One of the main features of these data sets is a similarity in the trends in catches at different fisheries. For example, catches were much higher at net and coble fisheries in the rivers Dee, Don, and Tweed during the late eighteenth and early nineteenth centuries than at any time since (Figs. 9.1, 9.2, and 9.4). Also, at most in-river fisheries and the newer sea fisheries, catches were much higher during the early 1870s and the 1880s than during the 1860s, the late 1870s or the 1910s (Figs. 9.2, 9.3 and 9.5). Catches obtained by the Berwick Salmon Fisheries Company (Fig. 9.4) are exceptional in this respect, as apparently are net and coble catches in the Dee (Fig. 9.1). However,

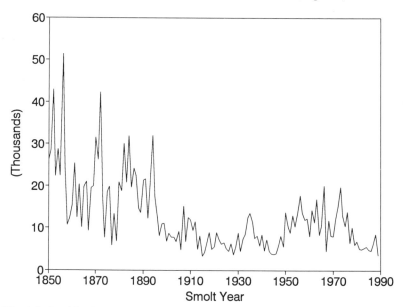

Fig. 9.3: Combined number of grilse and salmon caught from each smolt year at the Gordon Estate's 'Rake' net and coble fishery on the River Spey, 1850-1989.
Data: Crown Estate

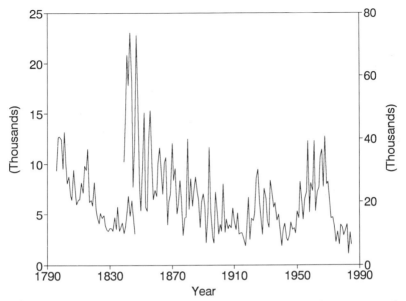

Fig. 9.4: The number of 130lb boxes of salmon shipped from Berwick-upon-Tweed each year, 1796-1846 (on left); and the combined number of grilse and salmon caught from each smolt year by the Berwick Salmon Fisheries Company's net and coble fishery, River Tweed, 1839-1985 (on right).
Data: Berwick Records Office MSS BRO 10/1 - Berwick Salmon Fisheries Co.

Summers (1992) considered that fishing effort by net and coble in the River Dee may have been reduced during the 1870s and 1880s when major engineering works were being undertaken at Aberdeen Harbour and so the catches presented may not be comparable with those obtained in later years.

The widespread nature of high catches in the early 1870s and late 1880s is evidenced by the fact that increased quantities of Scottish salmon were received at Billingsgate Market at these times (Anon 1901, p. *ix*) and catches are also known to have increased in the Severn, Avon and Stour, and Yorkshire districts in England (Anon 1902, Part III, Appendix Section I, pp. 4, 6 and 7) and in the River Rhine, Holland (de Groot 1991). At the fisheries from which data are presented, catches also rose again somewhat in the 1920s and 1930s (Figs. 9.2-9.5). This increase was also seen in the net and coble catch in the River Dee (Shearer 1985), for which data are only presented up to 1899 in this chapter, and in angling catches on the River Thurso (Shearer 1992). Catches fell everywhere to a low point in the 1940s whilst the 1950s to 1970s saw greatly increased catches at most of the surviving net and coble fisheries and in the sea fisheries. In the 1980s catches fell practically everywhere. (Comprehensive data covering all Scotland for the period 1952-1981 can be obtained in Anon [1983] and more recent data in DAFS—now SOAFD—annual *Statistical Bulletins* on Scottish salmon and sea trout catches.)

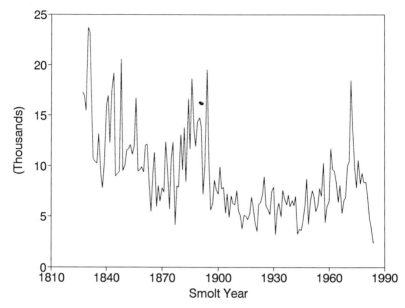

Fig. 9.5: Combined number of grilse and salmon caught from each smolt year at the
'Raik Sea' fixed net fishery in Aberdeen Bay, 1827-1984.
Data: Aberdeen Harbour Board

Interpretation of long-term fluctuations in catch numbers

It may not be wise to compare the high river catches seen before *ca.*1830
with catches obtained in later times, because of the introduction of new sea
fisheries, which intercepted fish which might otherwise have been caught in
rivers. However, the periods of high and low catches which have occurred
since the middle of the nineteenth century cannot be explained by changes in
the operation of the fisheries themselves (Summers 1992). Even during the
Second World War, when fishing effort was reduced, it is well documented
that salmon were scarce (e.g. Hutton 1947). These periods of high and low
availability of salmon must, therefore, represent real fluctuations in salmon
abundance resulting from factors affecting fish from widely differing rivers.

Since it would seem unlikely that geographically separate rivers would
experience similar fluctuations in their capacity to produce juvenile salmon,
it is likely that these common factors originate in the sea, where fish from
different rivers share a common environment (Hutton 1947).

Support for this hypothesis comes from historical changes in the marine
growth rate of salmon. When salmon numbers have been high, their
weight-at-age has also been high—indicating a link between growth and
survival. For example, Fig. 9.6 shows the mean weight of grilse caught
during July by nets in the River Spey between 1852 and 1991. From a
relatively low level, mean weights increased during the period *ca.*1870-1900,

then after about 1900 they maintained a lower level until about 1930. During the 1930s-50s they maintained a relatively steady level above that seen during the period 1900-1930, but from around 1960 a steady increase commenced, reaching a zenith in the early 1970s. During the 1980s they fell back to pre-1960 levels. It is likely that the mean weights recorded around 1970 were even higher in reality, because at that time fishermen tended to classify a significant proportion of the grilse catch as salmon, as a consequence of their larger size (Anon 1978). The increased sea-growth of grilse in the 1960s was not, of course, unique to Spey fish but was reported all around the United Kingdom and Ireland (Anon 1978; Browne 1986).

In further support of the hypothesis that marine influences have a broad effect on the numbers of salmon returning to widely differing rivers, it is known from the tagging of salmon smolts leaving the River North Esk (Angus) and rivers in western Ireland, that since the 1970s there has been an increase in natural marine mortality on salmon (Browne 1986; Shearer 1984). However, causes for these changes in marine mortality have not yet been identified.

Even more weight is added to this hypothesis if it can be shown that associations exist between changes in salmon numbers and growth rate and other changes in the marine environment.

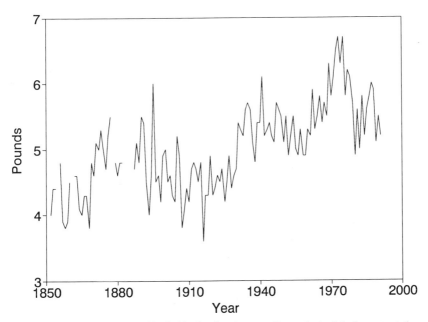

Fig. 9.6: The mean weight of individual grilse (ungutted) caught in July by nets at the mouth of the River Spey, 1852-1991. Data: Crown Estate

Historical changes in the marine environment in the North Atlantic

It is only recently that scientists have systematically collected data on sea surface temperatures, wind stress, salinity and so on. Changes in the marine environment during the nineteenth century can therefore only be inferred from historical information collected for different purposes or historical accounts. As with the interpretation of old catch statistics, the interpretation of such information is also an historical problem.

There have been major changes in the marine climate of the North Atlantic during the last two hundred years. During the late eighteenth century and in the early nineteenth century, relatively low temperatures prevailed over the entire area, as can be deduced from historical accounts of the abundance of sea-ice at Iceland (Fig. 9.7) as well as from the isotopic composition of glacier ice in Greenland and recorded air temperature data from England and Iceland (Dansgaard et al. 1975). In the 1840s sea-ice abundance at Iceland and Greenland decreased, but during the latter half of the nineteenth century it increased greatly again. Air temperatures in England also showed a temporary increase in the mid-nineteenth century (Dansgaard et al. 1975). The period ca.1920-1960 was anomalously warm compared to the average for the previous two hundred years. Ice abundance fell at Iceland and Greenland; sea surface temperature measurements showed a warming across practically the entire North Atlantic (Smed 1978). During the 1960s and 1970s there was a return to colder conditions. These have since ameliorated, but not to the extent of earlier in the century (Ellet and Blindheim 1992).

The changes in sea and air temperatures which have occurred during the period under review are the results of complex meteorological and hydrographic changes. Important factors are the strengths of the various ocean currents rather than direct heat exchange from the atmosphere, except in nearshore environments (Colebrook and Taylor 1979). For example, the strength of the warm North Atlantic Current is thought to be related to the strength of the prevailing westerly airflow over the North Atlantic (Martin 1972), and during the last 120 years changes in the annual frequency of westerly winds over the United Kingdom have broadly paralleled changes in North Atlantic temperatures (Cushing 1982). The frequency of westerly winds increased after ca.1900, falling again from the mid-century to the 1980s (Ellet and Blindheim 1992). Also, it is known that the cooling of the North Atlantic in the 1960s resulted from an increased northerly airflow over the Greenland Sea which resulted in the strengthening of cold surface currents down the eastern coasts of both Greenland and Iceland (Dickson et al. 1988b). Since the 1960s westerly wind stress over the North East Atlantic west of Britain appears to have increased and there has been a corresponding increase in sea state in the same area, perhaps because of the greater fetch of westerly winds (Carter and Draper 1988; Neu 1984).

These climatic changes have been mirrored by changes in the abundance of certain forms of marine life. For example, cod (*Gadus morhua* L.) were

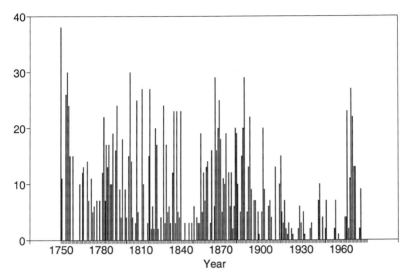

Fig. 9.7: An index of the abundance of sea-ice around the coast of Iceland (based on the length of coast affected and the duration of ice presence) 1750-1975.
Data: Lamb 1977

scarce at West Greenland throughout the nineteenth century, except for the 1840s, but there was a remarkable increase in the population during the 1920s as a result of an increased flow of Atlantic water up the West Greenland coast. The population collapsed during the 1960s when the cold East Greenland Current increased in strength (Cushing and Dickson 1976; Hansen and Hermann 1965; Jensen 1939). A similar fate also befell Barents Sea cod stocks during the twentieth century (Cushing and Dickson 1976).

Reports of salmon at West Greenland were infrequent during the nineteenth century, but during the period of twentieth century warming they appear to have been abundant. Moreover, salmon persisted at West Greenland during the 1960s and 1970s although the cod population collapsed (Dunbar and Thomson 1979).

The abundance of pilot whales (*Globicephala melaena* Traill) at the Faroe Islands (as ascertained by catches-per-unit effort) increased during the warming of the 1840s and between *ca.*1920 and 1960 (Hoydal 1985). Historical periods of high catches of spring spawning Norwegian herring (*Clupea harengus* L.) have also coincided with these warmer periods and large catches of herring (autumn spawners from the North Sea stock) have historically been obtained off the Bohuslän coast of western Sweden during cooler periods (e.g. 1760 to 1808 and 1877 to 1896) (Beverton and Lee 1965; Cushing and Dickson 1976).

Nearer to the United Kingdom, a great deal of information on biological changes has been accumulated by scientists during the twentieth century. For example, in the western English Channel during the 1930s, the concentration of phosphorus in winter decreased, the arrow worm *Sagitta elegans* (Verrill) was replaced by *Sagitta setosa* (J.Müller) and the abundance of all teleostean larvae decreased (except for the eggs and larvae of pilchards [*Sardina pilchardus* Walbaum] which increased). This situation persisted until the 1960s when things returned to what they had been in the 1920s (Russell 1973; Southward 1980). It has been suggested that the decrease in phosphorus concentration in the 1930s may have resulted from a decrease in the amount of deep water upwelling onto the European continental shelf. This could have been the result of a reduction in the quantity of deep ocean water being formed in the North West Atlantic due to the weakening of flow down from the Arctic, which in turn was a consequence of the atmospheric conditions which led to warming (Dunbar 1993).

Linked to the changes in the English Channel, which have become known as the "Russell Cycle" (Cushing 1982), has been a recent change in the migrations of mackerel (*Scomber scombrus* L.). The western mackerel stock spawns in spring in the Celtic Sea and feeds in summer in the northern North Sea. Little detail is known about migrations prior to the 1970s, except that in the 1960s the numbers which over-wintered off Cornwall increased greatly. During the late 1970s the mackerel left their feeding grounds in the North Sea in summer and migrated south through the Minches to over-winter off Cornwall. During the 1980s this pattern progressively changed with the mackerel now staying in the North Sea until winter, migrating outwith the Hebrides to the Celtic Sea and missing Cornwall (Corten and van de Kamp 1992; Lockwood 1988).

During the 1960s and early 1970s, a most striking change occurred in the North Sea: the populations of all of the gadoid species were augmented by several very large broods (occasioned by high juvenile survival). For example, haddock (*Melanogrammus aeglefinus* L.) recruitment had, since scientific investigations commenced in the 1920s, been what is now considered generally low (Holden 1978; Sahrhage and Wagner 1978) but in 1962, 1967, 1970, 1971, 1973, and 1974 there were large year classes; those in 1962 and 1967 being exceptionally large (Jones 1983). The growth rate of North Sea haddock also increased from before the Second World War until the 1970s, despite the fact that in the 1960s the population size, and hence intraspecific competition, increased (Cushing 1982).

The cause of the 'gadoid outburst', as it has become known, has never been satisfactorily explained. Dickson et al. (1973) found a negative correlation between cod recruitment and sea surface temperature, but Daan (1978) found exceptions to this. Cushing (1982) stated that increased gadoid recruitment occurred at a time when the timing of the spring plankton bloom in the North Sea was occurring several weeks later than it had done around 1950—a phenomenon which Dickson et al.(1988a) attributed to an increase in the frequency of northerly gales over the north east Atlantic and western North Sea. Cushing proposed a match/mismatch theory whereby larval gadoids might coincide with or miss the period of maximum zooplankton abundance. In the 1960s the two would have coincided. The basis of this hypothesis has recently been strengthened because of studies in Lofoten, Norway. It was found that the spawning of the copepod *Calanus finmarchicus* (Gunner), and hence the abundance of the copepodite stage I on which larval cod feed, is dependent on temperature, and can vary considerably in time of onset between years. Ellertsen et al. (1990) concluded that the match/mismatch theory may be the main cause of variable survival of cod larvae.

All the various events which occurred in the 1960s and 1970s—the North Sea gadoid outburst, the changes in the English Channel, the collapse of Greenland cold stocks and so on—were all in a sense related, owing to a broad climatic influence over a wide area, although there need not have been causal relationships between individual events in different areas.

Associations between salmon and changes in the marine environment

Over the last twenty or thirty years (the period for which most is known) there have been clear associations between changes in salmon numbers and marine changes. For example, low salmon mortality and the most rapid sea growth attained for at least 150 years coincided with the cooling of the North Atlantic in the 1960s, and with low mortality on gadoids and changes in the plankton fauna in the English Channel. During the 1980s salmon mortality increased and their growth rate decreased. At the same time some of the marine changes which occurred in the 1960s appeared to reverse; for example, decreased recruitment of gadoids and the change in mackerel migration patterns.

Looking back over the last 150 years, it can be seen that some of the periods of high and low salmon abundance before the 1960s may also have coincided with similar marine changes as occurred during the last 30 years. For example, around the 1880s, the North Atlantic appears to have become colder than it had been a few decades earlier (Fig. 9.7), and there was a relatively low frequency of westerly winds over Britain (Lamb 1977). The 1880s also saw a widespread increase in salmon numbers and sea growth—although sea growth then was not as rapid as around 1970. There are no real data available to demonstrate that biological changes occurred at sea in the 1880s, but it is known that pilot whale abundance at the Faroes was relatively low at that time, as it was after 1960, and that the Norwegian herring fishery collapsed around 1873. It is possible, therefore, that biological changes did take place in the 1880s.

If similar events took place in the 1880s as in the 1960s, then colder North Atlantic conditions resulting from a reduced westerly atmospheric influence and increased northerly influence may lead to better opportunities for salmon growth and survival. In order to give some credence to this hypothesis it would be useful to have some idea as to why such different conditions should affect salmon. However, little is known about the life of salmon at sea, especially in the first six months or so. In particular, it is not known where most mortality of salmon occurs.

It has been widely asserted that most mortality on salmon will occur within a short time of entry to the sea (Friedland and Reddin 1993), mortality being a function of the size of fish (Shearer 1984). This idea is supported by the fact that, in eastern Scotland, levels of natural marine mortality on sea trout (*Salmo trutta* L.) appear to parallel the levels of natural marine mortality on salmon. Catches of both species were large in the 1880s and 1960s (Summers 1992). Sea trout are thought to largely be a coastal species and they do not undertake pan-North-Atlantic migrations as salmon do. Since most mortality on east-coast sea trout must occur in the North Sea, it may be considered that most mortality on east-coast salmon should occur there also; the two species being similar in many respects (Summers 1992). Therefore, important influences may exist in the coastal environment. However, Summers (1992) also pointed out that, since natural marine mortality on salmon appears to have varied in a broadly similar manner in Scotland, England, Ireland, Brittany, and Holland, it would then appear likely that most mortality was taking place relatively far out in the north-east Atlantic, where fish from different rivers are sharing a common environment. Friedland and Reddin (1993) came to a similar conclusion for North American salmon, where they found that marine mortality similarly affected fish from rivers over a wide area of Atlantic Canada and New England, and that mortality was correlated with the rate of sea growth. They hypothesised that conditions during the first sea-winter were most critical in determining the numbers of returning adult salmon and challenged the idea that most mortality occurred near the shore. They also found that the areal extent of the north-west Atlantic Ocean which had a surface temperature of between 4 and 8 degrees Celsius in winter (which they considered to be the optimum habitat for salmon) has been correlated with marine survival rates on North American salmon over the last forty years.

Returning to European salmon, a way of reconciling the idea that much mortality may occur inshore with the idea that mortality may be occurring further out to sea, would be that salmon are influenced by phenomena which have widespread effects—affecting both the offshore and nearshore environment. This is entirely possible, since, as has been shown, diverse contemporaneous changes in the marine environment do occur and, though not directly related, may ultimately have a common cause. One phenomenon with a widespread effect which may have recently affected salmon survival has been the increase in sea state which has occurred across the north-east Atlantic between the 1960s and the 1980s (Carter and Draper 1988; Neu 1984). It is known that sea state can affect the survival of fauna living near the sea surface (Laevastu and Favorite 1988). Salmon have been found to swim near the surface of the sea most of the time, although they have been found to make rapid dives down to more than 150 metres (Jákupsstovu 1988), and mainly to eat surface dwelling organisms (Stasko et al. 1973). Therefore salmon may be particularly affected by factors which affect the abundance and ease of capture of organisms which live near the surface of the sea.

Conclusion—the relevance of historical studies of Scottish salmon catches

A recent decrease in the numbers of salmon entering Scottish rivers has caused alarm amongst salmon interests. This concern has been heightened because the biological mechanisms which have resulted in this decrease have not been isolated. It is, therefore, not possible to predict from recent scientific research what the future will hold for the Atlantic salmon.

However, historical studies show that there have been major fluctuations in salmon populations before. Conditions in the North Atlantic have varied greatly over the same historical period, and some of the changes observed in salmon catches have coincided with other marine changes. It seems likely that the marine environment has a major influence on salmon.

It may be concluded that further changes in the marine environment, which will inevitably occur, will result in corresponding changes in salmon populations. Although it is not possible to predict the form of future changes in salmon numbers, to be aware that the salmon resource is inherently variable is a fundamentally important fact of which all salmon fishery managers should be aware. When the recent increase in salmon mortality is viewed in this perspective, some hope is generated for the future. Therefore, in terms of the practical management of the Atlantic salmon, historical studies have possibly been more valuable than a host of research projects aimed at isolating specific mechanisms.

Bibliography:

Anon 1825. Reports from the Select Committee on the Salmon Fisheries of the United Kingdom. *House of Commons Papers (1825)*. 173 and 303, vol.v

Anon 1836. Reports from the Select Committee on Salmon Fisheries, Scotland. *House of Commons Papers (1836)*. 393, vol. xviii

Anon 1901. *Nineteenth Annual Report of the Fishery Board for Scotland, 1900. Part II: Report on Salmon Fisheries*. HMSO, London

Anon 1902. *Report of the Commissioners on Salmon Fisheries. Part III*. Cmnds. 1280 & 1281. HMSO, London

Anon 1978. *Triennial Review of Research 1976-1978*. DAFS Freshwater Fisheries Laboratory, Pitlochry

Anon 1983. *Scottish Salmon Catch Statistics 1952-1981*. HMSO, Edinburgh

Beverton R J H, Lee A J 1965. Hydrographic fluctuations in the North Atlantic Ocean and some biological consequences. In: Johnson C G, Smith L P (eds). *The Biological Significance of Climatic Changes in Britain*. Institute of Biology and Academic Press, London

Bielak A T, Power G 1988. Catch records - facts or myths? In: Mills D, Piggins D (eds) *Atlantic Salmon: Planning for the Future*. Croom Helm, London

Browne J 1986. The data available for analysis on the Irish salmon stock. In: Jenkins D, Shearer W M (eds.) *The Status of the Atlantic Salmon in Scotland* (ITE symposium no 15). Institute of Terrestrial Ecology, Abbots Ripton

Burnett J G 1951. *Powis Papers, 1507-1894*. Third Spalding Club, Aberdeen

Carter D T J, Draper L 1988. Has the north-east Atlantic become rougher? *Nature* 332: 494

Colebrook J M, Taylor A H 1979. Year-to-year changes in sea-surface temperature, North Atlantic and North Sea, 1948 to 1974. *Deep Sea Research* 26A: 825-50

Corten A, van de Kamp G 1992. Natural changes in pelagic fish stocks of the North Sea in the 1980s. *ICES Marine Science Symposia* 195: 402-17

Cushing D H 1982. *Climate and Fisheries.* Academic Press, London

Cushing D H, Dickson R R 1976. The biological response in the sea to climatic changes. *Adv.Mar.Biol.* 14: 1-122

Daan N 1978. Changes in cod stocks and cod fisheries in the North Sea. *Rapports et Proces-verbaux des Réunions.* Conseil International pour L'exploration de la Mer 172: 39-57

Dansgaard W, Johnsen S J, Reeh N, Gundestrup N, Clausen H B, Hammer C U 1975. Climatic changes, Norsemen and modern man. *Nature* 255: 24-28

de Groot S J 1991. Decline and fall of the Rhine salmon observed in the light of a possible rehabilitation. In: Mills D (ed.). *Strategies for the Rehabilitation of Salmon Rivers.* The Atlantic Salmon Trust, the Institute of Fisheries Management and the Linnean Society of London

Dickson R R, Kelly P M, Colebrook J M, Wooster W S, Cushing D H 1988a. Northerly winds and production in the eastern North Atlantic. *Journal of Plankton Research* 10: 151-69

Dickson R R, Meincke J, Malmberg S-A, Lee A J 1988b. The great salinity anomaly in the Northern North Atlantic 1968-1982. *Progress in Oceanography* 20: 103-151

Dickson R R, Pope J G, Holden M J 1973. Environmental influences on the survival of the North Sea cod. In: Blaxter J H S (ed.). *The Early Life History of Fish.* Springer-Verlag, Berlin

Dunbar M J 1993. The salmon at sea - oceanographic oscillations. In: Mills D (ed.) *Salmon in the Sea and New Enhancement Strategies.* Fishing News Books, Oxford.

Dunbar MJ, Thomson D H 1979. West Greenland salmon and climatic change. *Meddelelser om Grønland* 2022: 1-19

Ellertsen B, Fossum P, Solemdal P, Sundby S, Tilseth S 1990. Environmental influence on recruitment and biomass yields in the Norwegian Sea ecosystem. In: Sherman K, Alexander L M, Golds B D (eds.) *Large Marine Ecosystems.* AAAS, Washington

Ellet D J, Blindheim J 1992. Climate and hydrographic variability in the ICES area during the 1980s. *ICES Marine Science Symposia* 195: 11-31

Friedland K D, Reddin D G 1993. Marine survival of Atlantic salmon from indices of post-smolt growth and sea temperature. In: Mills D (ed.) *Salmon in the Sea and New Enhancement Strategies.* Fishing News Books, Oxford

Gee A S, Milner N J 1980. Analysis of 70 year catch statistics for Atlantic salmon (*Salmo salar*) in the River Wye and implications for management of stocks. *J.Appl.Ecol.* 17: 41-57

George A F 1982. Cyclical variations in the return migration of Scottish salmon by sea-age c1790 to 1976. MPhil. thesis, Open University, Milton Keynes

Hansen P M, Hermann F 1965. Effect of long-term temperature trends on occurrence of cod at West Greenland. *ICNAF Spec.Publ.* 6: 817-19

Holden M J 1978. Long-term changes in landings of fish from the North Sea. *Rapp.P.-v.Réun.Cons.int.Explor.Mer* 172: 11-26

Hoydal K 1985. Attempts to use the 274 years' Faroese time series of catches of pilot whales (*Globicephala melaena* Traill) to assess the state of the stock. ICES CM 1985/N:18

Hutton J A 1947. Salmon scarcity. An attempt to get at the real facts. *Salmon and Trout Magazine* 119: 55-62

Jákupsstovu S H i 1988. Exploitation and migration of salmon in Faroese waters. In:

Mills D, Piggins D (eds.) *Atlantic Salmon: Planning for the Future*. Croom Helm, London

Jensen Ad. S 1939. Concerning a change of climate during recent decades in the arctic and subarctic regions, from Greenland in the West to Eurasia in the East and contemporary biological and geophysical changes. *Det.Konglike Videnskabernes Selskab Biol.Medd.* 14(8)

Jones R 1983. The decline in herring and mackerel and the associated increase in other species in the North Sea. *FAO Fisheries Report* 291(2): 507-20

Laevastu T, Favorite F 1988. *Fishing and Stock Fluctuations*. Fishing News Books, Farnham

Lamb H H 1977. *Climate: Present, Past and Future. Volume 2: Climatic History and the Future*. Methuen, London

Lockwood S J 1988. *The Mackerel: its Biology, Assessment and Management of a Fishery*. Fishing News Books, Farnham

Martin J H A 1972. Marine climatic changes in the North-East Atlantic, 1900-1966. *Rapp.P.-v.Réun.Cons.int.Explor.Mer.* 162: 159-66

Martin J H A, Mitchell K A 1985. Influence of sea temperature upon the numbers of grilse and multi-sea-winter Atlantic salmon (*Salmo salar*) caught in the vicinity of the River Dee (Aberdeenshire). *Canadian J.Fish.Aquat.Sci.* 42: 1513-21

Menzies W J M, Smart G G J 1966. Salmon runs in Scotland. *Salmon Net* 2: 49-54

Mills D H 1987. Atlantic salmon management. In: Bailey R S, Parrish B B (eds.) *Developments in Fisheries Research in Scotland*. Fishing News Books, Farnham

Neu H J A 1984. Interannual variations and longer-term changes in the sea state of the North Atlantic from 1970 to 1982. *J.Geophysical Res.* 89: 6397-6402

Russell F S 1973. A summary of the observations on the occurrence of planktonic stages of fish off Plymouth 1924-1972. *J.Mar.Biol.Assn.UK* 53: 347-55

Sahrhage D, Wagner G 1978. On fluctuations in the haddock population of the North Sea. *Rapp.P.-v.Réun.Cons.int.Explor.Mer.* 172: 72-85

Shearer W M 1984. The natural mortality at sea for North Esk salmon. ICES CM 1984/M:23

Shearer W M 1985. Salmon catch statistics for the River Dee, 1952-83. In: Jenkins D (ed.) *The Biology and Management of the River Dee*. (ITE symposium no. 14). Institute of Terrestrial Ecology, Abbots Ripton

Shearer W M 1986. An evaluation of the data available to assess Scottish salmon stocks. In: Jenkins D, Shearer W M (eds.) *The Status of the Atlantic Salmon in Scotland* (ITE symposium no. 15). Institute of Terrestrial Ecology, Abbots Ripton

Shearer W M 1988. Long term changes in the timing and abundance of salmon catches in Scotland. ICES CM 1988/M:21

Shearer W M 1989. The River Tweed salmon and sea trout fisheries. In: Mills D (ed.). *Tweed towards 2000*. Tweed Foundation, Tweedmouth

Shearer W M 1992. *The Atlantic Salmon: Natural History, Exploitation and Future Management*. Fishing News Books, Oxford

Smed J 1978. Fluctuations in the temperature of the surface water in areas of the northern North Atlantic, 1876-1975. In: Proceedings of the Nordic Symposium on climatic changes and related problems. *Danish Meteorological Institute, Climatological Papers* 4: 205-11; Copenhagen

Southward A J 1980. The western English Channel - an inconstant ecosystem. *Nature* 285: 361-66

Stasko A B, Sutterlin A M, Rommel S A Jr, Elson P F 1973. Migration-orientation of Atlantic salmon (*Salmo salar* L.). *International Atlantic Salmon Foundation Special Publication Series* 4: 119-37

Summers D W 1989. The cruives of Don. *Salmon Net* 21: 21-28

Summers D W 1992. Studies of the Atlantic Salmon *(Salmo salar* L.*)* in Scotland. PhD thesis, University of Aberdeen

Taylor V R 1986. The early Atlantic salmon fishery in Newfoundland and Labrador. *Canadian Special Publications in Fisheries and Aquatic Sciences* 76

Thibault M 1991. Atlantic salmon annual catch statistics in France since the XIXth century. ICES CM 1991/M:16

Williamson R B 1991. *Salmon Fisheries in Scotland.* Atlantic Salmon Trust, Pitlochry

Acknowledgements:

I am very grateful to the following people and organisations who have permitted me to use data from their private records in this chapter: Mr Robert Clerk, Smiths Gore, Fochabers, on behalf of the Crown Estate Commissioners; Mr Ken Anderson, former director of the Berwick Salmon Fisheries Company; the Aberdeen Salmon Company; and Mr James Scott of Aberdeen Harbour Board. I also wish to thank Professor A D Hawkins of the SOAFD Marine Laboratory, Aberdeen, for commenting on a draft of the chapter.

10

MIDGES IN A CHANGING HIGHLAND ENVIRONMENT

Alasdair Roberts

This chapter aims to place the Highland midge *Culicoides impunctatus* in a historical perspective, presenting a progression of ideas based on information gathered from a variety of sources (Roberts 1993). Using quotations from literary texts (some of them written by scientists), I have argued previously (Roberts 1991) that midges were never mentioned in descriptions of the Highlands for the period 1750-1850 but featured regularly thereafter to the point of caricature: the subject lends itself to humour and holiday postcards. Going back beyond the period of the Highland tour, the same kind of negative evidence from Gaelic culture was further used to argue that the midge or *mheanbh-chuileag* (tiny fly) was not considered significant within the Highland environment. To answer one possible objection quickly, it is not possible to build up an immunity to midges by living with them; instead, it is visitors who may enjoy a few days free of attack.

Could there be a cultural explanation for the rather sudden change in what people wrote about the Highlands? The arrival of Queen Victoria at Balmoral encouraged a new interest in the moors and perhaps a new willingness to emphasise the hardships associated with shooting and fishing amidst rugged terrain. Despite this possibility, I remain convinced that a real change occurred in the environment of the Scottish Highlands which was associated with an actual rise in midge numbers. As will appear, I no longer believe that midges were continuously insignificant (far less absent) 'since prehistory' but I do see the nineteenth-century rise as an index, though hard to read, of environmental change. When all the changes implied by a shift from increasingly intensive arable farming and cattle-grazing (with the trans-humance of summer shieling) to the 'cleared' sheep walks and deer forests are considered, it begins to seem unlikely that midge populations could have remained unaffected. There is also the very important matter of climate to be considered, especially in the light of recent scientific work on midges (Hendry 1989; Blackwell et al. 1992a, b, c;).

To summarise the argument briefly, I am more convinced than ever that midge populations are now much higher than they were when Johnson and Boswell made their famous tour in 1772; that these can be related to environmental change in the West Highlands and Islands from the second half of the eighteenth century through to the first half of the nineteenth; and that with climate an additional factor the process of change was complex.

Science and Culicoides impunctatus

Of the thirty-four species of *Ceratopogonidae* or midge which are found in Scotland, the Highland midge *Culicoides impunctatus* far outnumbers the rest and is far more of a nuisance to man and livestock. These biting midges, distinguishable from the *Chiromonidae* which occupy the same general territory but scarcely bite, are found predominantly in areas where annual rainfall exceeds 50 inches, from the Atlantic coast to the mid-point of Scotland's mountains. Rainfall amounting to 208 inches fell on Lochaber in 1992 and 220 inches in 1990, but it has not so far proved possible to ascertain whether unusually wet summers are associated with higher or lower midge populations. The females seek their blood meals between May and September, swarming in conditions of reduced light at the beginning and end of the day when there is little wind. They breed particularly well in undrained areas of sphagnum moss and favour the shade and shelter provided by trees and bracken.

Since scientists began to visit the Highlands they have undertaken to record aspects of the Highland environment 'which have not hitherto been mention'd by the Learned', an attitude first expressed by the Skye steward and tutor Martin Martin, who emphasised the interest attaching to 'every Fiber of each Plant, and the least Particle of the smallest Insect' (Martin 1716, p *x*). The 'argument from silence' which has been questioned (see below) is therefore at its strongest in relation to the increasingly precise investigations of naturalists like Walker and Pennant in the 1760s through to the geologist MacCulloch in the early nineteenth century. Two more scientists may be used to underline the point. William MacGillivray spent a year in his native Harris in 1817 (Ralph 1993). His diary, soon to be published, shows MacGillivray's interest in flora and fauna developing into his particular specialism of ornithology. He explored the moors on a daily basis during August and September of 1817; nightly he recorded and speculated upon every natural phenomenon, including insects:

> We were assailed by winged Bugs, of what species I do not know, some of which I caught upon my skin. They did not bite, however, or at least not severely, for I did not detect many marks...[Starlings] frequent cattlefolds for the sake of the insects found among the dung. They sit on black cattle and sheep, probably to pick the insects... In regard to the object which I had in view on this trip, I may say that with the single exception of not having found specimens of the Itch insect I have attained them in a greater or less degree. (MacGillivray 1818)

'The itch', or scabies, was common among Highlanders. Elsewhere MacGillivray referred to bed bugs as 'light-armed cavalry' but was silent on midges. And as late as 1850 the entomologist H T Stainton was exploring the moors of Arran in search of the larvae of small moths (Stainton 1854, pp 104-11). Neither midge larvae nor swarms were recorded.

Midges have received surprisingly little attention from scientists in the present century. The impetus given by two post-war government surveys set up by the Secretary of State, Tom Johnston, with a view to reducing populations (Cameron et al. 1946, 1948) soon petered out, and midges were simply omitted from subsequent studies with titles of such apparent relevance as *Patterns of Highland Development* (Turnock 1970) and *The Organic Resources of Scotland: their Nature and Evolution* (Tivy 1974). On the other hand Frank Fraser Darling, in some respects the founding father of modern ecology in Scotland, was in no doubt about the harm done by *C. impunctatus* to tourism, agriculture and deer, exaggerating its effect to the point where 'every square yard of the Highland and Island moors has its midges' (Darling and Boyd 1964, p 117). He did not hold out any hope of a solution.

Recent research has brought midges back on to the scientific agenda, however, with the Agricultural Food Research Council and the Institute of Animal Health actively involved, although they have yet to publish their findings. Three papers have resulted from fieldwork being conducted on the west coast of Scotland by a team of entomologists and ecologists from the University of Aberdeen. The project is focused on the role of pheromones with a view to incorporating these chemicals into a control mechanism for midges: once the correct pheromone is identified it should prove possible to attract and destroy the biting female in swarms. Already this research has begun to yield precise data on the lifestyle of *C. impunctatus*. By applying the electron microscope to freeze-dried midges, painted gold, females have been shown to possess three times as many potential olfactory sensilla (or tactile hairs) on their antennae, reflecting their dependence on smell for the finding of blood meals (Blackwell et al. 1992a). Video camera has been used to establish individual flight patterns within midge swarms, as well as the size, shape and behaviour of swarms adjacent to breeding areas (Blackwell et al 1992b). Familiar generalisations, such as the tendency of midges to swarm before dusk in conditions of low wind, have thus been confirmed by observation of insects hitherto considered too small for the normal tracking and trapping techniques of entomology. Perhaps the most relevant evidence here, for its possible link with climatic change, concerns the negative effect of cold weather on the midge's twice-yearly breeding cycle (Blackwell et al 1992c).

Control of breeding was estimated to be at least ten years in the future until the recent announcement of a breakthrough: 'Scientists working in Argyllshire believe they have discovered the perfect midge bait, a chemical call sign emitted by the insects which alerts others to the prospect of a good meal... The researchers believe a synthetic version of the chemical, known as a recruiting pheromone, could be used to lure *C. impunctatus Goetghebuer* into traps by the million...' (*Sunday Times*, 13.6.93). Other points of potential interest to scientists are currently at the stage of press speculation fuelled by rumour. The discovery of a fossilised 70 million-year-old midge, with a red mite attached to it, has given rise to the claim that these mites might be parasitic on midges and the Aberdeen team has begun to collect these, although without any confidence that they could be useful in reducing midge populations. Similarly there has been a good deal of media attention paid to bats (Natterers, Pipistrelles) which, it is claimed, can consume a thousand midges in a night. Science remains properly sceptical, especially as to the feasibility of introducing bats as predators, but the historian must wonder whether the more heavily populated Highlands of the eighteenth century could have given house room to many more bats in the eaves and roof space of buildings.

The argument from silence

A good deal of written evidence is available for the second half of the eighteenth century and beyond, much of it published in book form: Johnson and Boswell (1773) are only the best known of many visitors to the Scottish Highlands recording their impressions for a wider public. This fashionable period for Highland tours produced accounts which ranged from the impressions of literary-minded diarists, artists and what would now be called travel-writers (Faujas de Saint-Fond 1784; Murray 1796; Leyden 1800; Wordsworth 1803; Southey 1819; Bowman 1825) to the precise records of naturalists and scientists (Pennant 1772; Walker 1808; MacCulloch 1819) culminating in the negative evidence of H T Stainton from his larvae hunt on Arran of 1850 (see above). Midges are nowhere mentioned. It might be thought that these genteel tourists avoided the moors which were later sought out by sportsmen, but in fact they went everywhere. The range of summer visitors includes Thomas Thornton, who gave readers an extended version of his game book in the 1780s. Thornton pursued a surprising variety of birds, beasts and fish in what, at this early date, was terrain largely unfrequented by sportsmen: 'July 26. Day charming. Went to some lochs... Said to be six miles off, but turned out ten. The day was too calm' (Youngson 1974, p 216). Twenty-seven trout were caught to provide a loch-side meal at the end of the day; no biting insects disturbed the sportsman or his ghillies.

Professor Christopher Smout is one of those who finds the argument from silence inconclusive. He has drawn attention to the fact that New England settlers failed to mention poison ivy although they were in fact troubled by it: 'Maybe in a world of great discomfort midges and poison ivy did not rank high on the list of human troubles' (Smout *pers comm.*). Dr George Hendry makes a similar observation to the effect that these same Highland diarists were silent on 'bed bugs, lice, horse-flies, stable-flies and mosquitoes... In an age of horse transport these travellers seem to complain about many things but never horse-borne insects' (Hendry 1992).

But in fact Pennant and Boswell both mentioned unidentified biting insects which were clearly not midges, while the poet James Hogg made specific reference to bed bugs: 'I got the best bed, but it ...was also inhabited by a number of little insects common enough in such places, and no sooner had I made a lodgement in their hereditary domains than I was attacked by a thousand strong' (Hogg 1804, p 81). Robert Burns used midges as a poetic image of country dancing while describing an evening on the banks of Loch Lomond: 'We flew at Bab the Bowster... like midges sporting in the mottie sun' (Brown 1973, p 9). Apparently Burns was not troubled by the biting variety on his Highland tour. In his more familiar Lowlands the midge was proverbial for its smallness (*Scottish National Dictionary* Vol. 5 1965, p 269) rather than in terms of blood-sucking swarms. The same is true, more remarkably, of Gaelic culture. Many sayings testify to the Gael's sensitivity to the natural environment, yet the *mheanbh-chuileag* was again celebrated for size, not biting, as in 'The cow is only a good deal bigger than the midge'.

An early example of the argument from silence, in English, is to be found inscribed on Timothy Pont's sixteenth-century map of Eddrachillis in north-west Scotland: 'All heir ar black flies in this wood ... seene souking me[n]s blood' (Stone 1989, p 30). Gaelic lore certainly registers an awareness of the black fly or cleg: 'The pithless poison is the fly's bite that stains the skin with blood' (Mackintosh 1819, p 161). A final example from an early period of biting insects which do not appear to have been midges is provided by the court poet John Taylor, who crossed the Mounth to Deeside on a misty summer evening in 1621. He found an inn, 'sup'd and went to bed, where I had not lain long but I was forced to rise, I was so stung with Irish musketaes, a creature that had 6 legs' (Taylor 1630). This is a puzzling example since 'Irish musketaes' sound like Highland midges, but it is not common to be attacked by them indoors after dark, as the quotation implies. Perhaps they were just mosquitoes.

Comparative documentary evidence

There are, however, two clear instances of midges in the first half of the eighteenth century. The first comes from Edward Burt, a military engineer who helped to build the first of the roads attributed to General Wade in the period around 1730. In all the detail of military correspondence and standing orders, covering everything from a relaxation in the saluting of officers to the procurement of ale for men advancing the roads a personal yard and a half per day (Taylor 1976, pp 32-45), no mention is made of anything equivalent to the repellents given to military personnel in mosquito-infested areas today (Hendry 1989, p 59; *pers comm* 1992).

However, following a discussion of Fort Augustus as the eastern limit of the heavy rainfall belt, Burt states:

> I have but one Thing more to take Notice of in relation to the Spot of which I have been so long speaking, and that is, I have been sometimes vexed with a little Plague (if I may use the Expression), but do not you think I am too grave upon the Subject; there are great Swarms of little Flies which the Natives call *Malhoulakins*.... These are so very small that, separately, they are but just perceptible and that is all; and, being of a blackish colour, when a number of them settle on the skin, they make it look as if it was dirty; there they bore with their little augers into the pores, and change the face from black to red. (Burt 1754, ii, 345)

The same climatic conditions applied then as now: 'They are only troublesome (I should say intolerable) in Summer, when there is a profound Calm; for the least Breath of Wind immediately disperses them; and the only Refuge from them is the House, into which I never knew them to enter.'

The second recorded instance is from August 1746. When Prince Charles Edward Stuart made his enforced tour of the Highlands and Islands after Culloden, he was bitten by *C. impunctatus* in Glenmoriston. According to one of his companions, John MacDonald of Borrodale, 'the evening being very calm and warm, we greatly suffered by mitches, a species of little creatures troublesome and numerous in the highlands' (Forbes 1896, iii, 379). The following June, the no-longer Bonnie Prince Charlie was in South Uist, sheltering under a sail in the heather near Loch Eynort. One of his party, John O'Sullivan, wrote an account of their ordeal: 'We were never a day or night without rain; the Prince was in a terrible condition, his legs & thy's cut all over from the bryers; the mitches or flys wch are terrible in yt contry, devored him, & made him scratch those scars, wch made him appear as if he was cover'd with ulsers' (Tayler 1938, p 193).

These early eighteenth century accounts are so recognisably *C. impunctatus* that my first instinct, on reading them, was to abandon the investigation. Even as a 'little Plague', Burt found midges 'intolerable' in the 1720s and 1730s; in the 1740s they were 'troublesome and numerous in the highlands' and 'terrible in yt contry' of the Outer Hebrides. But looked at in another way these early accounts throw the next period more clearly into relief, suggesting—powerfully—that the first half of the eighteenth century was a period of high midge populations in contrast to the following hundred years or so, when they were never mentioned although there were many more impressionable witnesses literate in English. No obvious environmental changes affected the Highlands around 1730—unless one counts a slow rise in population and a sharp rise in military road-building—so that one is left to consider the possible effect of a change in climate.

As is apparent to anyone who has been affected, an early evening midge attack is so dramatic as to be like no other form of insect bite or inconvenience. Continuing with the documentary evidence, I am much struck by the comparison between two experiences of the Highland environment. There is the 127-page midgeless disquisition on 'The Moors' by John Wilson (an Edinburgh professor whose pen name was Christopher North) based on a number of walking tours in the early nineteenth century. In one passage the emphasis is whimsically entomological, yet the only threat comes from ants:

> Go to a desert and clap your back against a cliff. Do you think yourself alone? What a ninny! Your great clumsy splay feet are bruising to death a batch of beetles. See that spider whom you have widowed, running up and down your elegant leg... Meanwhile your shoulders have crushed a colony of small red ants settled in a moss city beautifully roofed with lichens—and that accounts for the sharp tickling behind your ear, which you keep scratching, no Solomon, in ignorance of the cause of that effect. Should you sit down—we must draw a veil over your hurdies, which at the moment extinguish a fearful amount of animal life—creation may be said to groan under them; and insect as you are yourself you are defrauding millions of insects of their little day. All the while you are supposing yourself alone!... But the whole wilderness—as you choose to call it—is crawling with various life. (Wilson 1865 p 361).

The contrast with Charles Weld, writing a quarter of a century later, is sharp:

Talk of solitude on the moors!—why, every square yard contains a population of millions of these little harpies, that pump blood out of you with amazing savageness and insatiability. Where they come from is a puzzle. While you are in motion not one is visible, but when you stop a mist seems to curl about your feet and legs, rising, and at the same time expanding, until you become painfully sensible that the appearance is due to a cloud of gnats... I had no longer sat down than up rose millions of midges, which sent me reeling down the craggy steep, half mad. (Weld 1860 p 80).

As a final point on literary evidence (although one which is susceptible to a cultural explanation) it is interesting to note that midges are missing from Sir Walter Scott's *Waverley*, published in 1814, although they certainly feature in Robert Louis Stevenson's *Kidnapped* of 1886.

Climatic and other changes in the environment

Here my own research gives way to the knowledge and opinions of others in trying to find an explanation, or series of explanations, for fluctuating midge numbers. The Highlands and Islands of Scotland, situated on the Atlantic edge of Europe, are particularly sensitive to climatic change (Ch. 1 this vol.). A lowering of sea temperatures in the seventeenth century is believed to have brought down the Highland snow-line by as much as 400 metres (Lamb 1988 pp 156-7). Today midges breed as high as 1000 metres above sea level, so clearly this climatic change had the effect of greatly reducing the area available for breeding, and cold winters must have reduced the survival rate of midge larvae. Long before there was talk of global warming, temperatures rose during the opening years of the eighteenth century, suggesting an explanation for the consciousness of 'troublesome' midges in the period between about 1725 and 1746.

As another aspect of climate, westerly winds became more prevalent during the eighteenth century. Doctor Johnson was offered high winds in explanation of why there were no trees in the Hebrides, but it is perhaps pushing speculation a little far to suggest that midge populations were kept down by regular gales, just because swarms are quickly dispersed by wind of any strength. On another tack, however, it may be relevant to point out that it was easterly winds out of central Europe which brought the potato blight (*Phytophthora infestans*) to the Scottish Highlands (Lamb 1988, p 158) at precisely the time when, as I believe, midge populations were set to rise. The warm humid weather which favoured the spores of *P. infestans* was also ideal for *C. impunctatus*. Potato blight reached Scotland in 1846, and the same 'cool, rainy nights and moderately warm cloudy days' (Devine 1988, p 33) persisted into the high midge period.

One effect of colder summers and high winds at the end of the seventeenth century was to deal a further blow to the already much-depleted woodlands of north-west Scotland (Lamb 1977, p 466-7). By then the natural forest which once covered most of Scotland had been reduced to about 5 percent of the country's land surface due to a combination of climate, population pressure and external demand (Ch. 4 this volume).   Woodlands (or the lack of them) may be a factor in explaining the rise of *C. impunctatus*. In the eighteenth century the greatest Gaelic poet of his age Alasdair MacMhaighstir Alasdair called down a comprehensive list of biting insects on the head of the parish priest to justify his loathing for Eigneig in Moidart: 'Every beast that on me preyed, the wasp, the gadfly and the bee' (MacDonald 1924, p 275). Midges would surely have featured alongside clegs or gadflies (to say nothing of wasps and bees) if they had preyed on the inhabitants of Moidart then as they do now.

The Clanranald territories of Moidart and Arisaig still had extensive woods in the bard's time which extended to the borders of Lochaber. Even today what is left of the original forest cover has oak, birch, alder, ash, elm and native Scots pine sheltering a range of oceanic flora and vegetation including mosses and liverworts. Environmental change in this area came quickly: 'This transformation of Moidart and Arisaig into a short-term productive source of cheap wool and meat for urbanising and industrialising Britain was rapid and devastating. Little or no heed was now given to the protection of woodlands, and the marginal uses to which it was put were of less consequence to the landlord. A regime of continuous muirburn and deforestation was introduced' (Ch. 5 this vol. p 61). Arguably midges would not have flourished in the original complex eco-system with larvae a prey to other insects such as dragonflies, though the editor of this volume assures me that he has never been so badly bitten by midges as on a visit to the extensive semi-natural woodlands of Ardnamurchan immediately south of this area!

While the loss of natural woodland cannot be a general cause of rising midge population, most of the Highlands having lost forest cover by the sixteenth century, the well-managed Clanranald forest casts an interesting perspective on Moidart. Today government policy encourages mixed woodland as an alternative to the coniferous estates planted all over the Highlands since the 1920s. Forestry workers are badly afflicted by midges (Hendry 1989, p 41; *pers comm* 1992). Although the plantations themselves do not provide suitable breeding grounds for midges (or much else, due to the acidic effect of spruce needles) the element of shelter beside clearings and at the periphery may be relevant. Bracken also provides shelter, and has spread during the period associated here with rising midge numbers; the burning of heather in the interests of sheep ('muirburning') may be relevant in terms of a deteriorating Highland soil cover. Woodland was linked to ling by the poet Donnchadh Bàn: 'As I gazed on every side of me I could not but be sorrowful, for wood and heather have run out, nor live the men who flourished there' (MacLeoid 1952, p 390).

The combined effects of sheep and deer must be of crucial relevance to midges. The Highland Clearances have been debated in terms of economic history and emigration since their onset in the early nineteenth century, but only now are scholars beginning to address the possible ecological effects of putting sheep in place of people. A future ecological appraisal will have to consider carefully the position before the Clearances, drawing on the detailed information available from surveys such as that carried out by John Home in the summer of 1774 (Adam 1960). His account of Assynt conveys the impression of intensive arable farming near the coast and cattle farming inland, with the summer shielings, made fertile by cattle, increasingly used for corn. There are frequent references to woodland, which provided both shelter and grazing for cattle; none of the farm-by-farm 'observations' comments on midges. In the time of lowest midge incidence, as suggested here, an over-populated Highland region was drained and cultivated as never before, and in some areas the traditional export of black cattle to the Lowlands was supplemented by a greatly expanded trade in whisky for the industrial cities, with marginal and shieling land brought into cultivation (Gaffney 1960, p 29). Further drainage occurred, through the laborious construction of lazy beds, as potatoes were grown for subsistence.

Then came the Clearances, most famously at Strathnaver in the far north west in the opening decades of the nineteenth century. The environmental effects of depopulation and sheep-walks have been described in terms of 'a very minute investigation' for one Lochaber estate (Somers 1848, pp 126-36) close to the time when midges (it is here argued) appeared in greatly increased numbers. Six farmtowns, each formerly supporting ten or twelve families (double as many as in 1750 [Lang 1898, p 94]) were deserted, their furrows 'still visible amid the fern'; 40,000 sheep were clipped each year on one sheep-walk alone. Those people who remained were on the poorest land, their crops blighted by vapours emanating from the moor or moss. Meanwhile the possibilities of arable farming were demonstrated by a Fort William banker who 'commenced to drain, burn, lime, and cultivate his moss... Finer corn, turnips, and potato crops are nowhere to be seen.'

The crofters' historian James Hunter has argued that the former Highland agricultural system bequeathed to the new sheep farmers fertile areas of lowland ground along with upland pasture which had previously been grazed only in summer by cattle, and that 'purely extractive' sheep farming became the norm from the 1850s (Hunter 1973, p 204). A balanced view on the question of 'sheep-sick pastures', as debated in the 1870s, can be found in Chapter 7 (Mather, this volume), where the alleged destructive effect of sheep on woodland, there being so little of it in the first place, and the difficulty of finding reliable indicators for declining sheep performance are discussed. Nevertheless it appears that lambing percentages did decline in all areas of the West Highlands in the period under consideration, and that this was attributable to the deteriorating 'green land' of former shieling pastures rather than to the impact of sheep on heather 'black land'. Badenoch in the central Highlands appears to have been an exception—interestingly, since Scotland's leading collector of folklore from travelling people has identified this area as relatively midge-free (Henderson 1985). Mather does not mention midges, but emphasises the provisional state of knowledge on such key aspects of land management as heather burning. The intertwining of different environmental effects, in particular the difficulty of distinguishing the impact of sheep from that of red deer, is also discussed.

The environmental effects of deer on the Highlands are, again, much less well understood than their economic and social effects (see this volume,

Chapter 8). Thornton's 'very few deer seen' of the 1780s (and the earlier need to organise deer drives for sport) suggests small herds. By the 1880s deer had become a more economic proposition than sheep by at least 50 percent, and there were an estimated quarter of a million red deer in the Highlands by the middle years of this century. Sheep and deer now frequently share the same hill ground. Whatever their share of responsibility for a deteriorating environment, and whatever the consequent effect (if any) on midge-breeding areas, the presence of so many carbon-dioxide-breathing blood-meals can hardly have a negative effect on midge numbers. Deer forests (as indeed modern forestry plantations) are outside the scope of this investigation, but if the general argument is accepted then it is reasonable to infer that they have been a factor in the continuing rise of midge populations during the last hundred years.

Conclusion

The basic premise of this chapter is that midges, having been notably absent from the record during the previous hundred years, started to be reported around 1850—and that this reflected a real rise in their numbers. The rest is speculation, but it is encouraging to find that entomologists and ecologists are turning to the subject with renewed interest, and that the whole environmental movement is becoming involved with the Highlands of Scotland. It would be a pity, however, if the desire to preserve natural wilderness and bog were allowed to obscure the extent to which certain features of that wilderness have been created in the last two hundred years. At present the scientists engaged in fieldwork find it hard to imagine that the boggy ground of their investigations was ever different from today, and the ability of midges to travel considerable distances from their breeding grounds seems to cast doubt on the effect of drained and arable land before sheep. Climatic change finds more favour with specialists in the field (Hendry *pers comm* 1992) who nevertheless almost all agree on the value of a new perspective from history.

Emphasis has been placed here on a multi-factorial explanation of the phenomenon under consideration, requiring inter-disciplinary scholarship. But first the phenomenon has to be accepted. Given the many factors influencing a precarious Highland environment in the nineteenth century, it is actually harder to imagine there having been no effect on midges, although the midge-free period which started in the second half of the eighteenth century may also have been atypical in terms of what preceded it. Given the modern techniques of pollen analysis, and the first application of electron microscopes to these tiny insects, it may eventually prove possible to gather the kind of concrete evidence which convinces everybody. The fact that a fossilised midge has been found from 70 million years ago gives reason to hope that the insect traces which have begun to interest archaeologists may also become available for *C. impunctatus*. Meanwhile it would not be difficult to monitor the presence or absence of midges from different areas of the Highlands, summer by summer, and perhaps relate that to some of the variables which have been under discussion. This amounts to a practical as well as academic proposal which would benefit the tourists of tomorrow. There are still many unanswered questions surrounding the Highland midge, and these must surely be worth considering by the combined disciplines of environmental history.

Bibliography

Adam R J (ed) 1960. *Home's Survey of Assynt*. Scottish History Society, Edinburgh

Blackwell A, Mordue (Luntz) A J, Mordue W 1992a. Morphology of the antennae of two species of biting midge: *Culicoides impunctatus* (Goetghebuer) and *Culicoides nubeculosis* (Meigen) (Diptera, Ceratopogonidae). *J. Morphology* 213: 85-103

Blackwell A, Mordue (Luntz) A J, Young M R, Mordue W 1992b. The swarming behaviour of the Scottish biting midge, *Culicoides impunctatus* (Diptera: Ceratopogonidae). *Ecological Entomology* 17

Blackwell A, Mordue (Luntz) A J, Young M R, Mordue W 1992c. Bivoltinism, survival rates and reproductive characteristics of the Scottish biting midge *Culicoides impunctatus* (Diptera: Ceratopogonidae) in Scotland. *Bulletin of Entomological Research* 82

Boswell J 1773. *Journal of a Tour of the Hebrides*. Macmillan, London

Bowman J E 1825. *The Highlands and Islands*. Alan Sutton, London

Brown R L (ed) 1973. *Robert Burns's Tours of the Highlands and Stirlingshire 1787*. Boydell, Ipswich

Burt E 1754. *Letters from a Gentleman in the North of Scotland*. 2 vols. (1974 John Donald, Edinburgh)

Cameron A E et al. 1946. *A Survey of Scottish Midges*. HMSO, Edinburgh

Cameron A E et al. 1948. *The Second Report on the Control of Midges*. HMSO, Edinburgh

Darling F Fraser, Boyd J M 1964. *The Highlands and Islands*. Collins, London

Devine T M 1988. *The Great Highland Famine*. John Donald, Edinburgh

Faujas de Saint-Fond B 1784. *A Journey through England and Scotland to the Hebrides*. (1907 Hopkins, London)

Forbes R 1896. *The Lyon in Mourning*. 3 vols. (1975 James Thin, Edinburgh)

Gaffney V 1960. *The Lordship of Strathavon*. Spalding Society, Aberdeen

Gilpin W 1776. *Observations on the Highlands of Scotland*. (1973 Richmond, London)

Henderson H 1985. Letter to *The Scotsman* 4.9.1985

Hendry G 1989. *Midges in Scotland*. Aberdeen University Press, Aberdeen

Hogg J 1804. *A Journey through the Highlands and Western Isles*. (1981 Byways, Edinburgh)

Hunter J 1973. Sheep and deer: Highland sheep farming, 1850-1900. *Northern Scotland* i: 199-222

Johnson S 1773. *Journey to the Western Isles of Scotland*. (1907 Gardner, Paisley)

Lamb H H 1977. *Climatic History and the Future*. Methuen, London

Lamb H H 1988. *Weather, Climate and Human Affairs*. Methuen, London

Lang A (ed.) 1898. *The Highlands of Scotland in 1750*. Blackwood, Edinburgh

Leyden J 1800. *Journal of a Tour in the Highlands and Western Islands of Scotland*. Blackwood, Edinburgh

MacCulloch J 1819. *A Description of the Western Islands of Scotland, including the Isle of Man: comprising an Account of their Geological Structure; with remarks on their Agriculture, Scenery, and Antiquities*. 3 vols. Hurst, Robinson, London

MacDonald A, MacDonald A 1924. *The Poems of Alexander Macdonald*

(MacMhaighstir Alasdair). Northern Counties, Inverness

MacGillivray W 1818. *Journal of a Year's Residence in the Hebrides by William MacGillivray from 3rd August 1817 to 13th August 1818.* Aberdeen University Library: Special Collections MS 1033

Mackintosh D 1819. *Gaelic Proverbs and Familiar Phrases.* William Stewart, Edinburgh

MacLeoid A 1952. *Orain Donnchaidh Bhàin: The Songs of Duncan Ban Macintyre.* Scottish Academic Press, Edinburgh

Martin M 1716. *A Description of the Western Islands of Scotland.* (1981 James Thin, Edinburgh)

Murray S 1796. *A Companion and Useful Guide to the Beauties of Scotland.* (1982 Byways, Hawick)

Pennant T 1772. *Tour in Scotland.* Benjamin White, London

Ralph R 1993. *William MacGillivray.* HMSO, London

Roberts A 1991. Midges a modern scourge? The evidence of early accounts. *Review of Scottish Culture* 7.

Roberts A 1993. A rising cloud of midges in the Scottish Highlands. In: Butlin R A, Roberts N (eds.) forthcoming *Ecological Relations in Historical Times.*

Scottish National Dictionary. 1976. 10 vols. Edinburgh

Somers R 1848. *Letters from the Highlands on the Famine of 1846.* (1977 Melvens, Glasgow)

Southey R 1819. *Journal of a Tour in Scotland.* (1972 James Thin, Edinburgh)

Stainton H T 1854. *The Entomologist's Companion.* Reeve, London

Stone J C 1989. *The Pont Manuscript Maps of Scotland: Sixteenth Century Origins of a Blaeu Atlas.* Map Collector Publications, Tring

Tayler A, Tayler H 1938. *1745 and After.* Nelson, London

Taylor J 1630. *Pennyless Pilgrimage.* London

Taylor W 1976. *The Military Roads of Scotland.* David & Charles, London

Tivy J (ed) 1973. *The Organic Resources of Scotland: their Nature and Evolution.* Oliver & Boyd, Edinburgh

Turnock D 1970. *Patterns of Highland Development.* Macmillan, London

Walker J 1772. *Report on the Hebrides of 1764 and 1771.* (1980 John Donald, Edinburgh)

Walker J 1808. *An Economical History of the Hebrides and Highlands of Scotland.* 2 vols. Edinburgh

Weld C R 1860. *Two Months in the Highlands, Orcadia and Skye.* Longman, London

Wilson J 1865. *Recreations of Christopher North.* Blackwood, Edinburgh

Wordsworth D 1803. *Recollections of a Tour Made in Scotland.* (1974 James Thin, Edinburgh)

Youngson A J (ed) 1974. *Beyond the Highland Line: Three Journals of Travel in Eighteenth Century Scotland.* Collins, London

11

ENVIRONMENTAL CHANGE IN THE SAHEL
Lessons for Improving Resource Management within Marginal Agricultural Systems

Camilla Toulmin

Introduction

This chapter examines the marginal farming systems of the dry Sahel region of sub-Saharan Africa, and how they have coped with environmental change over recent decades. Its presentation within a book about Scotland serves two purposes:

(i) to demonstrate some of the common features of marginal farming systems in distant parts of the world, with the hope that their comparison casts light on our understanding of each one;

(ii) to throw into relief more general problems of interpreting evidence on environmental change, and the often strong assumptions which people bring to this exercise.

Changes in our perception of Sahelian farmers and how well they care for the land are examined, and the chapter concludes with the paradox that in the Sahel, poor and illiterate farmers are now seen as the best custodians of the countryside. By contrast, in Scotland and elsewhere in the European Community, our farmers are frequently seen as the despoilers of the natural environment, needing to be hedged about by state intervention.

The Sahel region of Africa

The word 'Sahel' comes from the Arabic, meaning 'shore', and describes the long ribbon of land which lies on the southern edge of the Sahara desert. It stretches over 7,000 km from the western tip of Senegal across to Somalia in the east. This ecological region, with annual rainfall of between 100 and 600 mm a year, is roughly 300 to 500 km in depth, and is an important transition zone between the arid Sahara to the north and the wetter savannahs to the south. The Sahel has been settled for many centuries, and criss-crossed by trading routes, migrating populations and military caravans. The cradle of great empires, such as Timbuktu, Wagadu, and the Almoravides, it now

Fig 11.1: The West African Sahel

supports a highly varied patchwork of farming and herding communities within a dozen independent nation states. The region is highly dependent on its land, water and vegetation for food, incomes, employment and exports. Choice of policies to support more sustainable land management has thus become a subject of major debate within government and donor circles.

This chapter will focus on the western Sahel region (Fig 11.1) made up of countries such as Senegal, Mali, Mauritania, Burkina Faso, Niger and Chad. These countries have a generally similar physical environment and climate, and comparable patterns of economic activity. They also inherit a common legacy from their colonial experience under the French, from whom they gained independence at the start of the 1960s. A particular common feature has been the nationalisation by all these governments in the years following independence of their natural resources, on the grounds that resources of such value need to be under the state's care. Since these administrations have rarely had the personnel, skills or finance necessary to manage these resources effectively, nationalisation has been highly damaging, breaking traditional controls over access to land, water and grazing and producing anarchic patterns of use and abuse. Fortunately, many governments are now making the first moves towards returning responsibility for land ownership and management to local communities.

Marginal farming systems in the Sahel

In common with marginal systems elsewhere, Sahelian farmers and herders are faced with certain challenges to which they must adapt. These include:

Great variability in rainfall
Grass and crop growth vary greatly, both from year to year and between

neighbouring areas in any single year. This variability promotes diversification of activity to protect incomes from risk, such as by cultivating different kinds of crop, herding a mix of cattle, sheep and goats, and combining agricultural with off-farm incomes, like crafts, hunting, and wage labour. It also encourages the development of social institutions which provide some insurance against risk to incomes and illness (such as large extended households) and many forms of mutual aid and co-operation between families. Such social support networks have also been described for traditional crofting communities in Scotland (Darling 1955).

Marked contrasts in moisture and resource availability on a broader regional scale.
As an example, the short rainy season brings the germination of highly nutritious grasses on the drier plains of the southern Sahara, but they only flourish briefly. Mobile pastoral production systems have evolved to take advantage of these seasonally available resources, with rainy-season camps being set up at which livestock are kept for several months, in a system not unlike that of the shieling (Fenton 1980). The differing comparative advantage of each ecological zone has encouraged strong trading links through which are exchanged Saharan salt and dates, Sahelian grain and livestock, and Savannah cotton and shea-nuts.

Weak levels of political and economic involvement at national level
This is due to relatively low levels of productivity, scattered patterns of settlement, and the difficulty with which such populations have been incorporated into broader market structures. This marginalisation has brought certain advantages, since farmers and herders have been very self-sufficient, providing for most of their needs, and thus less subject to external market pressures. Where the main function of government is to tax, rather than to re-distribute, distance from administrative centres confers a blessing. On the other hand, these regions have been neglected by national governments, local people have had no control over major decisions of great concern to them, and have witnessed the alienation of their more valuable resources by government or more powerful interest groups (Schoonmaker 1991). A similar picture of powerlessness in the face of decisions made by distant government is painted for Scotland's crofters (Hunter 1991).

Environmental change in the Sahel

Climate
Over the last 20,000 years, the Sahelian region has experienced great climatic change. From 20,000 to 12,000BP, a long dry period pushed sand dunes into many areas which are densely settled by farming peoples today. This period of aridity has been linked with the height of the Ice Age in the northern hemisphere (Nicholson and Flohn 1980). A wetter period from 10,000 to 4,500BP brought much more favourable conditions to the Sahara Desert. Rainfall through much of Africa south of the Sahara was then three

times its current volume. Fishing communities settled on lake shores in what is now parched land in southern Mauritania, while wild animals provided plentiful quarry for hunters, as elegant cave paintings from the Hoggar mountains of the central Sahara testify (Nicholson and Flohn 1980).

Since 4,500BP, conditions have deteriorated again, as can be seen from a study of changing water levels in the Lake Chad basin, at the eastern end of the region examined in this paper (Maley 1977), though the reasons for this drying up are not yet clear. Evidence from recent centuries describes patterns of drought and plenty, but with no marked trend in either direction. Travellers like Mungo Park, who crossed a large part of the Sahel in the 1790s, to map the course of the River Niger, described patterns of crop and livestock farming similar to those found today (Park 1799). Oral history and early Arab manuscripts provide similar evidence of occasional devastating drought mixed amongst years of greater or lesser abundance.

From the turn of this century, when rainfall records began in earnest, many years have seen rainfall markedly above or below the longer term average (Fig 11.2). The late 1940s and 1950s were abundantly wet, while since the late 1960s, the Sahel has experienced very dry conditions, with rainfall over the past twenty years some 25-30 percent below the average for this century. Interpretation of the Sahelian rainfall data is subject to considerable debate: first regarding whether such a decline is likely to continue; second the likely causes; and third the appropriate forms of action at local, national, and global levels to reverse or mitigate such adverse rainfall patterns. Opinion is still strongly divided as to the cause. Some argue

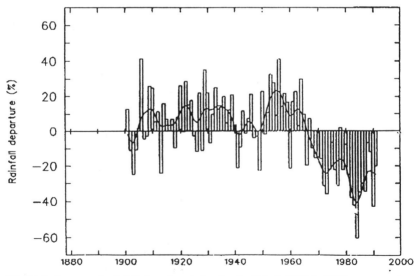

Fig 11.2: An annual rainfall departure index for the Sahel, 1901 to 1991, expressed as a percent departure from the 1951-80 mean. Up to 60 rainfall stations contributed to this regional series. (source: Hulme and Kelly 1992)

that it is probably the result of global warming, generated by CO_2 emissions from the industrial world (Hulme and Kelly 1992). If this is the case, there are few prospects of rainfall returning to higher levels in the foreseeable future. Others argue that local land use practices which remove vegetation and bare the soil are likely to be responsible, through increasing soil reflectance. A further view posits the existence of long term cycles of ocean temperature circulation which would also account for the rising levels of sea surface temperatures in the southern Atlantic.

So far as solutions are concerned, these differ according to likely cause. There have been calls by some African governments for compensation to be paid by the industrialised nations, given the adverse climatic conditions which Africa has suffered in recent decades and the assumed linkage with global warming. However, if changes in rainfall are due to natural cycles of thermal circulation in the oceans, there is little obvious action to take or compensation to be paid. In all cases, however, it would seem to make sense to encourage more careful management of soils and vegetation, both to make best use of what rain does fall, and to minimise any possible adverse feedback effect between land use and climate.

Changes in natural resources and their management
The impact of climate and human activity has provoked major changes in the distribution and productivity of natural resources in the Sahel. For example, annual grasses have replaced perennials in many grazing areas, tree populations betray a heavily skewed age structure with little natural regeneration taking place, and signs of soil erosion are evident in many farmers' fields. Wildlife populations and fish stocks have been decimated. Clearly, some of this change is due to humans, their hoes, ploughs, and livestock. Much of the change is also due to the decline in rainfall over the last 20 years.

Measuring and interpreting environmental change
The data available on environmental change are very patchy in their coverage, and are usually only available for a given site for a few years. It is very rare to have comparable data for the same site for a run of several decades, which is essential to assess longer term trends in an environment that experiences such great variability from year to year. Interpretation of the limited data which does exist is also complex, since one must try to disentangle the interlinked effects of natural and human-induced change. Given the inadequacy of the data available and their difficult interpretation, it is not surprising that a wide range of views are held regarding the nature of changes taking place, the relative importance of different causal factors, and what should be done. The two extreme ends of this range can be caricatured as the 'global pessimists' and the 'local optimists'.

At the *global* level, surveys of soil erosion and dryland degradation have been commissioned by the United Nations Environment Programme (UNEP). These data have formed the basis for discussion at the Earth Summit, held in Rio in June 1992, about the importance of land degradation in dryland areas, and the need for urgent action. Such data suggest major problems of soil erosion and resource degradation in dryland Africa, and elsewhere, with 70 percent of the world's dryland regions said to be suffering to a greater or lesser extent (UNEP 1991). These estimates are derived from the 'informed opinion' of experts. Humans are assigned the blame for such levels of environmental degradation, and costs of rehabilitation for these regions are estimated at many billions of dollars a year. Some observers consider it would be better to move populations out of these dry areas and re-settle them elsewhere.

In contrast to the global pessimists, the *local optimists'* argument is built upon a series of case studies of environmental change at local level from different parts of dryland Africa. These studies show the complexity of changes taking place, and demonstrate the resilience of physical systems and patterns of production in the face of substantial rainfall variability (Mortimore 1989; Toulmin 1992). Rainfall—its volume and timing—is shown to be the motor for a highly dynamic ecological system that exhibits no tendency to return to a particular equilibrium (Hiernaux 1992; Behnke and Scoones 1992). Such studies do not assert that no degradation is taking place, nor that it is of negligible importance. Rather, they emphasise the great capacity for creative adaptation amongst human societies faced with environmental change. They stress the need to take a localised approach, examining the nature of degradation in that particular context and its major causes, so that appropriate solutions can be found in collaboration with local people.

Perceptions of environmental degradation in dryland Africa have been dominated by the idea of 'desertification'—an ungainly term which has served to spread confusion and misunderstanding. For a long time, it was thought that the Sahara (amongst other deserts) was steadily advancing, bringing waves of sand rolling down to engulf more fertile areas. Recent detailed research shows this picture to be false (Helldén 1991). Instead, a continuous process of soil and vegetation degradation is occurring in more densely settled lands, rendering crop and livestock systems less productive and more vulnerable to recurrent droughts. Desertification is now taken as 'land degradation in dryland environments due to a mixture of human and climatic factors'. A new Global Convention to Combat Desertification is being drawn up for signature in June 1994, in which special attention will be paid to promoting more careful husbandry of soils and vegetation, through marriage of local skills in managing these resources with the knowledge of outside researchers and extension agents.

Encouraging *participation* by local land users in the planning and design of project interventions is now a central plank of most initiatives in the Sahel. This builds upon the heady rhetoric employed by many governments across the region, which emphasises putting power back into the hands of farmers and herders, and making them responsible for the management of their own land. However, old approaches are hard to change. Many administrators now talk of the need to 'make people participate', which usually means 'I tell you what to do, and you participate'. Even government planners with the best of intentions feel confused and frustrated in their attempts to involve local people more fully in development projects, since no-one quite knows how to do it.

New methods are now being tried out to get planners and farmers talking together—using maps of the village's lands drawn in the sand, diagrams constructed from stones, twigs, and leaves to investigate which trees villagers prefer and why, game playing and theatre workshops—to stimulate discussion of how problems of poverty and environmental management might best be tackled. These methods are helping to transform the traditional power relations between highly centralised government structures, and local people. At a recent village workshop in Mali, using such methods, a farmer remarked —'It's quite astonishing to see you outsiders walking about our fields and willing to discuss our problems. Normally, people from the government don't visit our village and, when they do, they don't get out of the car. Sometimes we wondered if they had legs at all!'

The Sahelian farmer: natural custodian of the countryside?

Development strategies in the Sahel have pursued a bewildering variety of approaches, illustrated by the jargon used by development experts in this and past decades. We have moved from integrated rural development projects, and plans to combat desertification to more recent emphasis on village level land use planning, people's participation, and provision of basic needs. The production of jargon has been kept in business by outside observers and development experts, who engage in endless dialogue about the correct approach to achieving sustainable development in the Sahel. Local Sahelian populations are notable by their absence from such debates and have been the patient recipients of each prescription from this 'laboratory of development alchemy' (Cross 1990).

Fortunately, debate about the right approach to Sahelian development seems now to have taken a more promising direction. We have moved in the last fifteen years from a situation in which the farmer or herder was characterised as a devastator of the environment, responsible for massive damage, and needing strict control through government agents, to the perception that local farmers and herders are often the best able to conserve the natural resources upon which their own livelihoods depend. This change in perception has come about because it is clear that government control over land use and resource management has been a massive failure. At the same time, many of the development projects undertaken by western agencies have been markedly unsuccessful. By contrast, detailed research has demonstrated the complexity and sophistication of many 'traditional' farming practices. Increased attention is being paid to how best to incorporate local knowledge into development programmes in future.

It is now recognised that where rights over land are uncertain, farmers have no incentive to improve their holdings. The main donor agencies have been pushing for reform of land tenure and decentralisation, to allow land to be formally managed by village councils or herders' associations, instead of remaining in government hands. Government also plans to change laws relating to tree ownership. Until now, farmers have had to pay for a permit to prune, or cut down a tree, even one which they have planted themselves. At the same time, charcoal makers have been able to buy permits conferring rights to cut wood on land that farmers consider their own. Instead of conserving woodland, government policy has discouraged new plantings, since few farmers have the time to plant, water and protect tree seedlings unless they can be sure to harvest them one day.

For Ali Coulibaly, a farmer near the large market town of Ségou, in central Mali, changes in the law are long overdue.

> You can't call a tree your own. I found a wood cutter on my land the other day with an axe. When I told him to clear off, he produced a piece of paper from the government, entitling him to cut wood, or so he said. I took him to the local forest office where they confirmed that he had the right to cut a cartload of wood. So he was in the right and I was in the wrong. You can be sure that he'd slipped the official a packet of cigarettes beforehand.

A reversal in thinking about traditional farming practices is also taking place. Local farmers are increasingly perceived as the best custodians of the country's natural resources, often knowing better than outsiders how to use the land sustainably. Scientists reluctantly admit that it is not easy to understand and predict how Africa's drylands behave. Many development projects are now trying to build on farmers' knowledge of their own immediate environment.

A development worker in one of the many non-governmental organisations that have sprung up all over the Sahel in the last few years, explains what they do:

> We call it the "cafeteria" approach to rural development. Instead of having a set menu, we offer the farmer a variety of possible techniques to adopt. It's for them to choose what seems right for their particular circumstances.

At the national forestry research station in Mali, known in the past for training para-military forestry guards, the Director Harouna Yossi stresses how far thinking has changed:

> In the past we thought we knew what people wanted and made choices for them, not even bothering to ask for their views. The results have been very disappointing. We have wasted the last thirty years doing research which is of no interest to farmers. Now we must encourage farmers to tell us where their main problems lie so that future research produces useful results.

Conclusions

From this brief overview of change within the Sahel, three questions arise which may be of relevance to the situation in Scotland:

What is the right distribution of power and responsibility between land users and government? In the Sahelian case, it has swung from one extreme to the other—from government assuming all power and responsibility for land planning and management, to a radical decentralisation of such responsibilities to local level committees. What role does this leave for the government to play? Clearly, there are certain limited essential tasks for any administration to provide, in terms of maintaining the rule of law, and providing firm, fair and rapid enforcement of property rights, where these are brought into dispute. Balancing local versus national interests is also the due preserve of government, as when herders in a drought-struck region of the country need to gain access to better grazing resources elsewhere.

How can a more effective partnership be established between local land users and outside technical experts? Local farmers and herders in the Sahel have a considerable body of knowledge and experience about how things work within their particular environment. Scientists and technicians, who are usually trained in a single discipline, frequently only value formal systems of knowledge, and have little respect for the broader and more practical knowledge built up by farmers. Mutual contempt has characterised most contacts between farmers and experts. Yet both parties have much to offer the other. A major constraint to such effective partnership from the Sahelian experience has been inability of western trained scientists and extension workers to listen to and value the knowledge and perceptions of illiterate farmers and herders. Field-based training workshops in participatory planning and research methods have begun to address such issues with considerable success.

How is our interpretation of environmental change influenced by an underlying agenda? Global pessimists and local optimists start from very different viewpoints regarding the evidence available on environmental change, which leads to markedly different strategies to be pursued. Such strategies range, on the one hand, from large scale global programmes to combat desertification, concentrating effort on satellite monitoring of soils and vegetation, and emphasising the role of high technology in solving problems of land degradation. On the other hand, many observers refute the importance of technical fixes, and stress the importance of policies aimed at re-establishing responsibility and powers amongst land users themselves, empowering them with the information needed to develop systems of crop and livestock production which better conserve the resource on which they and their grandchildren must depend.

In the Sahelian region of West Africa, as in Scotland, the interpretation of environmental change provokes hot debate, because people have different visions of the past, based partly on the evidence available, but also partly on the myth of a golden age, brought to ruin by colonial conquest and the economic forces unleashed, and to which we are unable now to return. Careful analysis is essential to clarify the current incidence and trends in different forms of resource degradation, and to identify the major causes of environmental degradation. Such an analysis needs a strong historical dimension in order to demonstrate the underlying physical forces at work within the landscape.

Bibliography

Behnke R, Scoones I 199. Re-thinking range ecology: Implications for rangeland management in Africa. *Dryland Networks Programme Issues Paper* 33. IIED, London

Cross N 1990. *The Sahel: The Peoples' Right to Development.* Minority Rights Group, London

Darling F Fraser (ed.) 1955. *West Highland Survey: An Essay in Human Ecology.* Oxford.

Fenton A 1980. The traditional pastoral economy. In: Parry M L, Slater T R (eds.) *The Making of the Scottish Countryside.* Croom Helm, London

Helldén U 1991. Desertification: Time for an assessment. *Ambio* 20 (8).

Hiernaux P 1992. In: Stenseth N Chr, Lusigi W (eds.). *Proceedings of the Oslo Meeting on Economy-Ecology Interactions in the Sahel.* Centre for Development and the Environment, University of Oslo, Norway

Hulme M, Kelly M 1992. *Linkages between Climate Change and Desertification with Particular Emphasis on the African Sahel.* Paper prepared for the Overseas Development Administration. Climatic Research Unit, Norwich.

Hunter J 1991. *The Claim of Crofting: The Scottish Highlands and Islands, 1930-1990.* Mainstream, Edinburgh

Maley J 1977. Paleoclimates of Central Sahara during the early Holocene. *Nature* 269: 573-77.

Mortimore M 1989. *Adapting to Drought: Farmers, Famines and Desertification in West Africa.* Cambridge

Nicholson S, Flohn H 1980. African environmental and climatic changes and the general atmospheric circulation in late Pleistocene and Holocene. *Climatic Change* 2: 313-48

Park M 1799. *Travels into the Interior of Africa.* London

Schoonmaker K 1991. Mbegué: The disingenuous destruction of a Sahelian forest. *Dryland Networks Programme Issues Paper* 29. IIED, London

Toulmin C 1992. *Cattle, Women, and Wells: Managing Household Survival in the Sahel.* Oxford.

UNEP 1991. *Status of Desertification and Implementation of the United Nations Plan of Action to Combat Desertification.* United Nations Environment Programme, Nairobi

INDEX